Economics for Busy People

The Most Useful Science You're (Probably) Not Using

Cameron M. Belt

EconomicsFor

Book Cover by Cameron M. Belt

First edition 2026

Contents

For my grandfather, David Arlington Freeman (1943-2023).

He was never too busy.

Without him, I wouldn't be an economist.

Love and Prayers.

Introduction: Is That Thing Alive?

Quite The Shock

A few years ago, I found myself face to face (if you can call it that) with a live razor clam.

I'd honestly never seen one before.

I was staring at the shell when suddenly, slowly, it cracked open. To my shock, this long, off-white "thing" slid out.

My mind raced with questions. "What is *that*? Is that thing alive? Is it safe to eat?" But most importantly: "What is *that* doing *here*?"

What shocked me wasn't seeing a new sea creature. It was where I was sitting when I saw it.

I was in a sushi bar, behind a 7/11, in a suburban strip mall, in Las Vegas...300 miles from the closest ocean.

Why Was I Surprised?

I shouldn't have been surprised for two reasons.

First, I've lived in Las Vegas all my life. Growing up here, you see things that should shock you every day. Medieval knights fighting in castles next to pyramids, across from a Statue of Liberty surrounded by a roller coaster—all under billboards featuring showgirls, magicians, and chefs.

In comparison, a live razor clam isn't that shocking.

Second, I'm an economist. I've spent my career studying how we all come together to make each other's lives better in ways no one expects or plans. Fresh sushi in the desert shouldn't surprise me. And yet it did, because knowing and experiencing are two very different things.

It's one thing to understand how economics works. It's entirely different to see and feel the magic of economics playing out right in front of your face.

You might be asking: "What does the most boring subject in the world have to do with sushi in the desert?"

Short answer? Everything.

How Fresh Fish Gets to the Desert

That clam's journey to my table is a remarkable story of human cooperation. And it happens millions of times every day without anyone being in charge.

It started in Japan, where someone I'll never meet spent years learning to harvest these clams from cold ocean waters. They got up before dawn, worked in dangerous conditions, and perfected skills most of us couldn't imagine developing.

Within hours of being scooped from the ocean, that clam was packed in ice and rushed to an airport. A pilot then flew it, along with other cargo, across the world.

At the Vegas airport, freight handlers moved it through customs and onto refrigerated trucks. The trucking company took it to a distributor. The distributor sent their own trucks out to the restaurant.

Meanwhile, the sushi chef had spent years perfecting his craft. He built relationships with suppliers and created a reputation that made customers willing to pay $8 for a single piece of clam.

In about 24 hours, this clam went from the ocean in Japan to the cold case in front of me.

Nobody planned this. No "Foodie Commission" decreed that Vegas should have world-class sushi. No government agency designed the optimal clam transportation network. Yet thousands of strangers across the globe cooperated to deliver exactly what I didn't even know I wanted. And I had economics to thank for it all.

From Experiencing to Understanding

Right now, whether you like it or not, you're experiencing economics every day. But, like I said, experiencing something and understanding it are completely different things.

Many people go through life simply reacting to what happens in the economy without knowing why it's happening, what it means, or how they might influence it.

This book is about changing that. It's about taking you from just experiencing economics to understanding, and hopefully using, it.

The goal isn't to turn you into an economist. It's to help you think like one when it matters. This is all so that you can see the patterns, expect the consequences, and make choices that align with how the world works rather than how we wish it worked.

Why Should Busy People Care About Economics?

I get it. You're busy with work, family, errands, bills, health, and trying to find time to relax. But the reason you're busy is because you care deeply about your life. You work hard to provide for and take care of your loved ones.

That care and love for your family and community is exactly why understanding economics matters so much.

Economics affects everything you value: your job security, your family's opportunities, your community's prosperity, your country's future. Understanding how it works gives you clearer thinking about decisions that shape all of these.

Here's what I find fascinating. Economics is probably the most useful subject available to all of us. It can sharpen every decision we make about money, time, risk, opportunity, even how we vote. But almost nobody uses it. Not because it's too hard. But, because it's been presented in a way that makes it feel irrelevant.

Most people think economics is only about complicated formulas, confusing charts, and debates that seem to not matter in everyday life.

In reality, economics is the study of how we act, make decisions, and work together in a world where we can't have everything we want. It explains why we make trade-offs, how our choices reveal what we value, and why outcomes often differ from intentions.

Economics won't tell you what to think. But it will give you a framework for thinking more clearly. And once you begin to think like an economist, you'll see the world in a whole new way.

How This Book Works

This book won't teach you how to calculate GDP or read a Fed report. Other books do that well (see the Further Reading section). This book instead focuses on how to think about the underlying relationships and truths within the economy.

Understanding a few key ideas (like scarcity, value, trade, and the cost of time) can help you understand how our world works better than any equation or talking head on television will.

Each chapter is clear, short, and practical. Each starts with "One Takeaway" and ends with a "Bottom Line" that capture the key ideas.

My hope is you can start this book over Saturday morning coffee and begin using these ideas by Monday. Let's get busy.

Why Do We Need Economics?

Before we start, we need the right foundation. Most people think economics is about money, markets, or government policy. But before we can understand any of those things, we need to understand what economics studies. Hint: it starts with you.

Chapter One

We Are The Subjects Of Economics

One Takeaway

Economics studies how we all act, make choices, and work together in the real world.

What Economics Is All About

Most people already have an idea or opinion of what economics is. Chances are if you ask a room of ten people to define it, you'll end up with ten different definitions (twelve if any of them are economists).

Some say it's about money. Others say it's about resources, wealth, or maybe incentives. Some simply say it's about "the economy," without explaining what that means. None of these answers are entirely wrong, but none quite get to the core, either.

Here's a better way to put it: **economics studies how we all act, make choices, and work together in the real world.**

At the fluffy, abstract level, economics is the science of **human action**. It starts with the simple fact that people act with purpose to improve their lives as they see fit. These improvements require time, energy, and resources that are limited and that others want too. It looks at the process of our choices, and how those choices ripple out in a world filled with other people.

Anytime you weigh options or trade one thing for another, you're practicing the logic of economics. In fact, if you've ever asked yourself, "Is this worth my time, money, effort, etc.?" you're already thinking like an economist.

Why This Matters

The goal of every science is to make sense of the world we live in. Understanding how people make decisions isn't just for academics. It's for everyone. Whether you're a plumber, teacher, IT guy, or someone running a household, thinking like an economist can help you focus on what matters.

This isn't just about theory or lines on a blackboard. It's about survival. In the long run, the wealth of our family, friends, and communities depends on understanding how decisions are made, how trade-offs work, and what happens when cooperation between people breaks down. When the ideas of economics are misunderstood, or ignored, entire societies can drift into slow growth, waste, or ruin.

The good news? The basics aren't difficult. What is difficult is being consistent and remembering the basics in a fast-moving, complex world. That's where the real challenge, and the real insight, lie.

Where Economics Begins

Economics is built around a few foundational truths:

- **People have endless wants and goals, but limited resources to get them.**
- **Everyone wants to improve their situation in their own way.**

- **We make trade-offs every day because every choice comes with a cost.**
- **We don't act alone.**
- **Time is a factor in our decisions and actions.**
- **Rules and systems matter.**

These may sound simple, but they're powerful. They explain why things happen the way they do, and how things could be better.

Judgment-Free Zone

Economics doesn't tell you what your wants or goals should be. It takes your wants and goals as given and asks if your actions align with them. That means economists shouldn't be concerned with casting judgment on what you want and value.

The fact is, each of us is different. We have different knowledge, different resources, and we want different things. None of our differences make us better or worse than anyone else.

If one person uses $5,000 to go on a vacation and the other uses the same amount to start a business, neither is "right" or "wrong." What matters is the basic fact that each person has their own wants. They were each willing to give up something they had to get closer to something else they wanted.

This kind of thinking asks simple but useful questions, such as:

- What is it that you want or value (your ends)?
- What resources, information, and limits do you have (your means)?
- What are you willing to give up to get what you value (your costs)?

After this, you can better understand if your choices are helping you or holding you back. That then leads to questions like:

- Are your actions helping you get what you value or not?
- Can you get what you want by giving up less?
- How does what you value complement or conflict with what others value?
- Do your choices lead to any costs you didn't expect?

The Bottom Line

Economics offers a way of thinking that helps us deal with the real world. It gives us the tools to understand trade-offs, see unintended consequences, and appreciate systems and rules that make cooperation and progress with others possible. The basics are simple. Learning to think this way, even just a teeny bit, can change how you see the world.

Chapter Two

We Aren't Rocks (Or Chemicals, Or Atoms)

One Takeaway

The economy isn't a machine. It's the result of real people making real choices. To understand the big picture, always start with the individual.

Real People in the Real World

Individual choices aren't random. For example, let's say a person chooses to save instead of spend. Or maybe they start a business instead of staying at a job. Or even move across the country for better opportunities. Each action involves an intentional decision. These decisions are what drive the economy.

That's what makes economics different from the natural sciences. In physics, things fall from trees. In chemistry, elements combine. But in the economy, people act and choose.

Rocks don't weigh trade-offs. Chemicals don't change their behavior based on current events. But humans do. Every day. That's why understanding the real world means starting with real people and how they act.

Different Subjects

We all likely took a science class at some point in our lives. Whether it was biology, chemistry, or physics, these subjects are known as natural sciences. The natural sciences study forces that are (mostly) predictable and consistent. Gravity doesn't care about your values. Electrons don't change course because they read a headline. These systems are stable. They don't think, and they don't adapt.

People, by contrast, are constantly making choices based on what they know, what they expect, and what they care about. We adjust. We hesitate. We get things wrong and then try something else. **And this makes human behavior fundamentally different from patterns we see in the natural sciences.** Because of this, we can't treat people like predictable rocks.

This difference isn't just philosophical. Knowing this sets the stage for how we understand and study economic problems and solutions. You can't predict human action the way you predict a chemical reaction. You can't control an economy the way you control a machine. And you can't solve social problems by treating people like objects that respond mechanically to inputs.

Individuals Drive Outcomes

When we talk about "the economy growing" or "the government spending," we're using shortcuts. Markets don't move themselves. Governments don't make decisions. People do.

Behind every policy, every price change, every business success or failure, you'll find people making decisions with their own values, knowledge, and limits in mind.

That's why economics focuses on the individual. Because trying to explain big outcomes without understanding the small decisions behind them is like trying to explain a forest without explaining what trees are.

An Example: How a Coffee Shop Opens

Consider something as simple as a new coffee shop opening in your neighborhood. The local news might report it as "retail expansion creates new jobs." But that misses the real story.

Behind that coffee shop is Jane, who worked at Starbucks for five years and noticed her customers always complained about long lines and impersonal service. She decided the neighborhood needed something different. Her decision wasn't random, it was purposeful.

But Jane's choice set off a chain of other individual decisions:

- A local contractor agreed to renovate the space because the job paid well and fit his schedule.
- A supplier chose to deliver beans and pastries because Jane offered good terms.
- A college student took a part-time job there because the hours worked with her class schedule.
- Neighbors started buying coffee there instead of driving to the chain store because they preferred the atmosphere.

Each person made their own choice based on their situation. No one coordinated them. No committee decided the neighborhood needed a coffee shop. It happened because individuals, each driven by their own goals, found ways to cooperate that made everyone better off.

These actions did create jobs. That's true. But headlines are only important so long as we remember they are the result of our actions.

Why This Matters

Understanding that people are different from rocks sounds silly, but it helps explain the insights that follow in this book like:

- Why we can work together with millions of strangers without anyone being in charge
- Why one-size-fits-all policies rarely work as intended
- Why growth comes from individuals trying, failing, and trying again

This perspective, that people are different than rocks, grounds us. It reminds us that social trends aren't the result of abstract forces or collective moods. They're the result of people like you and me making trade-offs, acting off of what we know, and trying to do the best we can with what we've got.

The Bottom Line

People aren't particles, rocks, or chemicals. We don't move on fixed paths. We choose, we adapt, and we act with purpose. Understanding the economy means understanding the people who create it. We each have our own goals, constraints, and decisions. This is why economic science is so important. We need a science that takes these facts into account rather than assume them away.

Why Do We Act, Choose, And Change?

Now that we know economics is about people, not equations or models, we can dig in. If human action is the starting point of all economic thinking, then we need to understand why people act in the first place. What drives us to choose one thing over another? What makes us change our minds? The answers reveal the logic behind every decision we make. Even if our decisions seem illogical.

Chapter Three

We Always Act For A Reason

One Takeaway

Economics starts with the simple fact that humans act with a goal in mind.

What Is Human Action?

Human action is the starting point of economics. Simply put, **humans act with purpose**. Every action is made with a specific future outcome in mind.

This simple concept forms the basis of economic thought. By reminding ourselves that human action is always purposeful, we can begin to understand the decisions people make, the trade-offs they consider, and the systems they create.

It's important to note, **acting with purpose does not mean acting perfectly**. In many cases, people believe a certain action will lead to a specific outcome, but they may be wrong (more on this later).

Why Does This Matter?

Economics deals with intentional, voluntary behavior. People act in an effort to improve their lives in some way. **But, not all actions are purposeful**. Things like breathing or blinking, which occur without intent, aren't the focus of economics.

Focusing on purposeful action allows us to look deep into our lives. For example, why does someone choose to spend their savings on a vacation instead of investing in the stock market? Both are purposeful actions. They're both attempts at improving some specific situation. But even though they are both purposeful, they are both different.

Different motivations and trade-offs shape each decision. Understanding this helps us better understand not only individual choices but also the broader effects they create.

Action Comes in Many Forms

Sometimes our actions are driven by earning money. That's often true, but also only a part of the story. People also act to find joy, increase comfort, climb the social ladder, or even find personal meaning. All of these can be drivers of action.

Economics seeks to create a clear picture about the logic behind choice. Whether someone starts their own business, volunteers their time, plants a garden, or buys a fancy car, each of these actions reflects individual judgment on what will improve their life.

Every decision has a purpose. Those purposes are based on people trying, in their own way, to the best of their knowledge and ability, to make their lives better.

Key Principles of Action

This first principle of economics is a building block that enables us to look deeper. We can add onto this first truth with other truths such as:

1. We act based on voluntary choices to achieve specific ends.

2. We generally prefer more of a good thing to less.

3. We generally prefer to receive things sooner rather than later.

4. We expect to benefit from trade, otherwise we wouldn't agree to the trade.

From here, we begin to have a path to understand the logic behind our actions and the actions of others. This is especially useful when we begin to see actions or outcomes from others that we find strange or counterintuitive. What we may see as counterintuitive behavior is often still purposeful behavior.

The Bottom Line

Economics begins with the simple fact that humans act purposefully. Every choice we make is an attempt to improve our situation—even when we get it wrong. By recognizing that people act with purpose, we gain a powerful lens to understand the real world, not as a set of random outcomes, but as the product of billions of individual decisions unfolding in front of our eyes.

Chapter Four

We Don't Like The Same Things, And That's Good

One Takeaway

Value is in the eyes of the beholder. This allows people to trade and cooperate with each other, leaving each other better off.

What is Value?

Value exists only in our minds. Nothing in the world has value unless someone believes it has the potential to bring satisfaction, fulfill a desire, or fit a need. One person might love a piece of art, another may see it as clutter. A meal that one person loves may be disgusting to another. These differences highlight why a standard agreed-upon worth for any good or service is a myth.

An object's features, no matter how unique, do not make the object valuable on their own. Value is always determined by how an individual perceives something's usefulness in helping them achieve their own goals.

Because value is personal, economists call it **subjective value**. The opposite idea, that value is built into the object itself, is called **objective value**.

Value is Not Set in Stone

Value can not only be different between different people, but it can also change based on individual circumstances, new knowledge, and even likes or dislikes. A personal story illustrates this well:

While at a crowded pub outside London, I saw a man buy four pints of beer at £3 each. His friend left him to carry all four through the crowded room—a near-impossible task. Realizing he couldn't manage all four and unwilling to risk leaving one behind, the man with four pints offered me one of the beers for £1. I gladly accepted the trade.

Even though he had just paid £3 for the beer, its value to him changed within moments. The effort and risk of holding onto it were too costly, so he reduced the value of this fourth beer (the beer intended for the friend who abandoned him) and struck a deal with me. This shows how value can shift depending on time and constraints.

What Affects Value?

People value things differently for various reasons:

1. **Preferences**: Personal tastes differ. What's appealing to one may be disgusting to another.

2. **Expectations**: People's ideas about the future influence how they value goods today.

3. **Knowledge**: Awareness of a good's uses or benefits determines its perceived value.

4. **Circumstances**: Context and urgency play a huge role, as seen in the pub example.

Imagine there's a root or plant right now in the Amazon rainforest that has the potential to treat cancer, obesity, HIV, blindness, and deafness simultaneously. If no one knows about it, or how to use it safely, it holds no value. Even with its incredible potential, the absence of knowledge, expectations, and plans to use it makes it worthless.

Value in Trade

People having differences in what they value is one of the main reasons trade exists. When two people choose to buy or sell to each other, it's because each one values what they're getting more than what they're giving up.

Imagine someone trading a sandwich for a soda. The person who wants the sandwich is hungrier than they are thirsty. The person who wants the soda is thirstier than they are hungry. When they trade, each person walks away with something they value more. **Nothing new was created, yet both are better off**. Boom. As my wife says, "double happiness."

The more we differ in what we value, the more opportunities and reasons we have to work with one another. What might seem useless to one person can be highly valuable to someone else.

Can We Measure Satisfaction?

Because value is personal, so is satisfaction. One person might get a lot of joy from a simple cup of coffee, while another barely notices the flavor. But here's the challenge: even if both people could rate their satisfaction on a scale of 1 to 10, there's no way to know whether one person's "7" is greater or lesser than the other's "5." These numbers don't map onto anything concrete or comparable. The same goes for dissatisfaction, or even pain. Someone's "5" on a pain scale could be a "10" on someone else's.

Satisfaction lives only in the mind of the person experiencing it. It can't be measured, added up, or compared across people. Because of this, we must recognize that each person is the best judge of their own satisfaction.

The Bottom Line

Value lives in the mind of each individual. Because we value things differently, we have a pretty good reason to trade and cooperate. But that same difference also means we can't measure or compare satisfaction across people. The goal of economics isn't to calculate how happy people are. It's to understand how they act on what they value and why that matters.

Chapter Five

We Can't Have Everything, So We Have To Choose

One Takeaway

Scarcity forces choices. Economics begins with understanding how we prioritize what matters most when we can't have it all.

What is Scarcity?

At the core of economics lies another undeniable truth: **we can't have everything that we want.** There are never enough resources, time, money, or energy, to satisfy all our desires. This is **scarcity**. It's a basic fact of reality and it makes choice necessary.

Scarcity means that when we use something for one purpose, we give up the chance to use it for something else. Every decision we make involves a trade-off. Scarcity forces us to choose.

For example, consider a farmer deciding whether to plant soybeans or corn on his land. The farmer cannot use the land for both crops at the same time. The farmer must choose one.

What is a Good?

When we talk about things people choose between, we call them **goods**. A good is anything that someone believes can help them achieve an end—whether that's staying warm, enjoying a meal, relaxing, or earning money. Goods aren't defined by what they are, but instead by how someone values them.

But not everything useful is a good. For something to be a good, it must be both useful and scarce. That's why air, while essential to life, usually isn't a good in economic terms. As of this moment here on Earth, we don't need to choose how to use it. It's freely available (at least in most places). Economics focuses on things that are scarce and worth choosing between.

How Do We Deal with Scarcity?

Because we can't have everything, we have to prioritize. This process—of weighing costs, benefits, and trade-offs—is called **economizing**. We constantly make decisions about how to use our time, money, energy, and attention to achieve the outcomes we want.

This isn't limited to money. It applies to all resources. Time is scarce. Energy is scarce, even mental focus and attention is scarce.

Why This Matters

Scarcity might seem obvious, but it's another reason why economics exists. Without scarcity:

- Prices wouldn't exist—we wouldn't need to compare or prioritize goods.

- Trade-offs wouldn't exist—we wouldn't need to choose between options.

- Competition wouldn't exist—there'd be no struggle over limited resources.
- Policy would be easy—there'd be no limits or consequences to weigh.

We wouldn't need to pay much attention to our choices if we lived in a magical world without scarcity. It'd be great if we lived in that world, but we don't. In our world, policies have trade offs. Every decision you make has a cost. And every time we use a resource it means it isn't used on something else.

Scarcity Doesn't Guarantee Value

Just because something is scarce doesn't mean it's valuable. Scarcity matters *only when* something is also useful or desired. You could own the only crate of VHS tapes in the world, but that doesn't mean anyone wants them. Value comes from scarcity and purpose, both **how useful something is** and **how much people want it.**

The Bottom Line

We can't do everything, have everything, or be everywhere, so we have to choose. Goods are the things we believe can help us achieve our goals. When we recognize scarcity as an undeniable starting point, we begin to see how every decision shapes the world around us.

Chapter Six

We Act Purposefully, Not Perfectly

One Takeaway

People act with intention, but not always with precision. Understanding the difference helps explain why mistakes, surprises, and change are needed for progress.

How We Act

Every action you take has a goal and a plan to get there. Economists call these goals, "**ends**," and the tools or steps you use to reach them, "**means**." Whether it's choosing a career, cooking dinner, or trying a new marketing strategy, you're acting to bring about a future you believe is better than your present.

This doesn't mean you'll always succeed, but it does mean you're aiming at something.

Why We Need Plans

Action is always future-oriented. We act because we expect that doing something—anything—will make our future better. To do that, we form mental blueprints: What do I want? What do I have? What can I do with what I have to get what I want?

Without a plan, there's no action. Even something as routine as making breakfast requires a series of deliberate steps: What's in the fridge? How hungry am I? Do I have time to cook, or should I grab a granola bar?

Every action reflects a trade-off: time, effort, money, or attention. When you act, you're making a choice. **Every choice says something about what you value in that moment.**

Purpose Is Not Perfection

We don't always get it right. Sometimes the plans and means we choose don't work. Plans fail. Circumstances change. We misjudge what's possible or misunderstand what others want. So long as you acted with a defined end in sight, and chose means you believed would get you there you are acting not only purposefully, but also **rationally**.

A business launches a product that doesn't sell. A student picks a major they later regret. A friend books a vacation that turns out to be a hassle. These aren't irrational actions; they're purposeful actions that didn't produce the expected result.

The key is that purposeful and rational don't mean perfect. It means people act based on what they believe will work, using the information and resources they have. That's enough to build a solid economic understanding of the world.

An Example

Imagine someone spends their last $20 on a lottery ticket instead of groceries. To an outsider, that may seem irrational. They may know how slim the odds are of any single person walking away from the lottery as a winner. But from the buyer's perspective, the potential for a life-changing win outweighs the certainty of maybe a bite to eat.

This is rational action. It's based on personal goals and limited means. It may not work, and there may be other choices that might have a better chance of working, but it was chosen for a reason. Economics doesn't have to agree with the ends. It just needs to understand how and why people pursue them.

What We Learn from Mistakes

When plans fail, they teach us something. A failed product, a missed opportunity, or a bad investment reveals a gap between what we expected and what happened. That's not a flaw in the system; it's the system working. Real-world feedback helps us adjust. We refine our plans. Then we try again.

This constant back-and-forth between goals and results is how progress happens in the real world.

Why This Matters

When we understand that purposeful action doesn't mean perfect action we become better decision-makers and more thoughtful observers of the world around us. We begin to ask questions like:

- Are my goals clear?
- Am I using the right tools or strategies to reach them?

- What can I learn from what didn't go as planned?

This way of thinking helps us look past the surface of someone's actions—including our own. Instead of asking, "Why would they do that?" we ask, **"What were they trying to achieve?"** That subtle change creates empathy, clearer thinking, and better responses towards others.

The Bottom Line

We don't act randomly. We act with purpose. This is true even when we miss the mark. Understanding this difference between intention and perfection helps us make sense of success, failure, and everything in between. It also reminds us that good economics starts by asking: *What were they trying to do, not simply why were they doing that?*

Chapter Seven

Short Answer: We Want To Improve Our Lives

It Started With a Cup of Coffee

If you're a busy person like me, chances are you probably bought a coffee this morning. Maybe you didn't think much about it. But that single decision, the one you make almost every day without noticing, demonstrates everything this section just taught you.

You acted with purpose when you bought that coffee. You weren't randomly wandering when you ended up at the counter. You wanted something. Maybe you needed the energy. Or a cup of coffee brings you comfort and a moment to yourself before the day starts. That want drove you through the door. Every human action starts the same way: with a person trying to make their situation better than it was a moment ago.

Your choice was yours alone. You ordered an oat milk latte. Your coworker, like me, gets a basic, boring black drip. Your boss skips coffee entirely and drinks tea. No one here is wrong. A month ago, you might have thought there was an objectively "best" coffee order and wondered why everyone doesn't just get that. Now you understand that value lives in each person's mind, not in the drink itself.

You faced scarcity. You had $5 and fifteen minutes. You couldn't have the $7 specialty pour-over and make your 8:00 meeting. So, you chose. The latte gave you what you wanted most within the constraints you had. You didn't solve an equation. You made a trade-off.

And you acted purposefully, not perfectly. Last Tuesday you were running late and grabbed gas station coffee you didn't even like. That wasn't irrational. It was the best option available given what you knew and what you had at that moment. The fact that you regretted it later doesn't mean the decision was wrong. It just means your circumstances made every option imperfect.

Here's the useful part about what the ideas in this section offer. You'll start catching yourself making choices on autopilot. I'm not just talking about coffee, but about how you spend your lunch hour, where you put your energy at work, what you do with your weekends. And you'll start asking yourself: am I choosing this because it's good, or just because it's familiar? What am I actually giving up?

Those questions sound simple. But most people never ask them. You will now. And it starts tomorrow morning, at the counter, with a cup of coffee.

How Do We Make Decisions In The Real World?

In the real world, we don't make decisions in isolation or with perfect information. We face limits, competing priorities, and changing circumstances. So how do we actually navigate these daily choices? How do we decide what's worth our attention, when to cut our losses, and whether the next step is worth taking? These practical questions shape every decision we make.

EconomicsFor

Chapter Eight

We Ask "Does It Work?" Before "Can We Do It Better?"

One Takeaway

Before you fine-tune a process, make sure it actually works. Effectiveness first. Efficiency second.

What's Rational?

For someone to act rationally it simply means they act with some goal in mind, using what they have to try to get to that goal. It doesn't mean people act with calculated perfection (see Ch. 6). But what happens after we act? That's where effectiveness and efficiency come in.

Effectiveness Comes First

Effectiveness means your plan actually does what you hoped it would do. If you're launching a product or building a nonprofit, step one is **whether**

you did what you were trying to do.

If your actions didn't get you where you wanted, then maybe you were chasing the wrong outcome or using the wrong tools. That's a failure to align means with ends. It means you weren't effective.

For example, let's say a small restaurant, "Joe's Cafe," wants to increase customers. They could spend months perfecting their social media strategy. They optimize posting times and create beautiful content. Every one of their posts goes viral. There's no wasted effort on getting customers interested. But if their food simply doesn't taste good because they lack good recipes, all that social media work won't matter. The first question is: do people actually enjoy eating here?

That is Step 1.

Then We Talk About Efficiency

Efficiency becomes important when something is already effective. That's when we can ask, "Could we get the same job done with less?" Less time, less money, fewer headaches.

It's a second step—not the starting point.

That's because trying to make an ineffective plan more efficient is like getting really good at rowing a boat that has a hole in it. You might row faster, but you're still going to sink.

Once Joe's Cafe proves their recipes work and customers are coming back for the food, *then* they can focus on efficiency: reducing wait times, streamlining the ordering process, or finding ways to serve more customers with the same staff. They're optimizing a system that already works rather than trying to perfect something that's fundamentally flawed.

Why This Matters

In personal life, business, and policymaking, people often get this backwards. We can optimize what doesn't work. We fine-tune broken systems.

We measure performance before checking if our goals are even clear.

Rational action doesn't mean perfect outcomes. But it does require that we evaluate whether our plans are working, and whether we're learning from what doesn't.

That's where real progress happens. Not from perfection, but from doing → learning → refining → repeating.

The Bottom Line

Start with a clear goal. Test whether your plan gets you there. If it does—great. Now look for ways to improve. If it doesn't—don't optimize. Re-evaluate. Efficiency is only worth chasing once you know if you are going in the right direction.

Chapter Nine

We Rank What Matters Most

One Takeaway

Every choice you make reflects what you value most in that moment, but how much more you value one thing over another can't be measured because it can always change.

Choices Reveal Our Priorities

When you make a choice—what to eat, how to spend your evening, where to invest your time—you're doing more than picking an option. You're revealing your internal ranking of preferences at that moment.

Some economists call this a **value scale**: a mental ordering of what matters most to you, based on what you believe will improve your situation.

Let's say you spend your Saturday night at a concert instead of watching Netflix or attending a friend's game night. That decision tells us the concert was your top priority at that moment. But here's the key: **we can't measure how much more you valued it than the other options.**

There's no scale to say the concert brought you "three times more happiness" than staying home. All we can know is the choice revealed your highest-ranked option at that time.

Why Value Can't Be Measured

Value exists only in the mind. You can rank your preferences—A over B over C—but you can't assign them objective scores. You might love chocolate ice cream more than vanilla, but you can't say it gives you "6.3 more units of joy." That kind of precision doesn't exist outside of spreadsheets and simulations.

What's more, we can't compare value between people. If Jack spends his morning running and Jill spends hers reading, we can't say one is "better off" than the other. Each acted according to their own value scale, shaped by their unique goals, preferences, and experiences.

How Preferences Shift

Value scales aren't fixed. They shift constantly in response to new information, changing tastes, or environments.

- If you find out the concert's headliner canceled, maybe Netflix jumps to the top.
- If your neighbor adds a last-minute guest to game night, that might change your plans again.
- If your priorities shift—say, you're feeling sick or a surprise bill pops up—your value scale adjusts with them.

This ability to change is what makes human behavior so dynamic, and why it's so hard (impossible) to predict perfectly.

Why This Helps You Make Better Choices

Most of us don't think about our own value scales. We just act and hope it works out. But once you see that every choice reflects a ranking, and that the ranking can shift, you gain something surprisingly practical: the ability to catch yourself.

Have you ever committed to something and then dreaded it as the day approached? That's your value scale shifting after the decision.

The concert sounded great on Tuesday. By Saturday, rest and relaxation moved up the ranking and the concert moved down. You didn't make a bad decision. Your priorities changed. Understanding that gives you **permission to adjust** rather than force yourself through something that no longer sits at the top of your list.

It also helps explain disagreements. When someone makes a choice you wouldn't make — how they spend their money, how they raise their kids, what they do with their weekends — the base reaction is to assume they're wrong. But they're acting on a value scale you can't see. Their ranking reflects experiences, priorities, and trade-offs you may know nothing about. **You don't have to agree with their choices to understand that those choices make sense from where they sit.**

The Bottom Line

Our choices reveal what we value most in the moment. That ranking changes as life changes. Understanding this encourages **empathy** and a deeper appreciation for the many ways people go after happiness and satisfaction.

Chapter Ten

We Get Nothing For Free

One Takeaway

Every decision comes at the cost of the next best alternative. Even if that cost is invisible.

What Is Opportunity Cost?

Maybe you've heard the saying, "There's no such thing as a free lunch." It's not just a clever phrase telling you to be distrustful of free offers—it's one of the most important ideas in economics. Whenever you choose one thing, you give up something else. That "something else" is called your **opportunity cost.**

But unlike a price tag, opportunity costs aren't always clearly seen. They're often hidden, untouchable, or easy to overlook. They might take the form of time you can't get back, energy you could have spent elsewhere, or a missed chance you never even considered.

What You Give Up Matters

Imagine you're offered free tickets to a concert. Sounds like a win, right?

But what else could you have done with that evening? Maybe dinner with a friend. A workout you've been meaning to get to. Or just a quiet night of rest. The tickets may be free, but your time—and what else you could've done with it—isn't.

The same is true for money. If you spend $50 on a concert, you don't just lose the $50. You lose whatever else that money could have done for you. A nice meal. A step closer to a savings goal. An online course. That trade-off is your opportunity cost.

The Broken Window

Here's a classic story that makes this idea stick. A kid throws a rock through a bakery window. A crowd gathers. Someone shrugs and says, "Well, at least the window maker gets paid. That's good for the economy."

On the surface, that's true. The window maker earns money. He spends it somewhere else. Activity ripples outward.

But here's what nobody sees. The baker had been saving to buy a new oven. Now that money goes to replacing a window instead. The oven maker gets nothing. The bakery doesn't grow. The baker's customers don't get more options.

The window replacement is visible. The oven that was never bought is invisible. But both are real. One happened. The other didn't and now never will.

This is opportunity cost applied to the world around you. Every dollar spent fixing a problem is a dollar that can't be spent building something new. Economic activity, money changing hands, is not the same thing as economic progress. The next time someone points to spending as proof that things are going well, ask yourself: what would that money have done if it hadn't been spent on a broken window?

Why It's Easy to Miss

Opportunity cost is often invisible. We don't usually stop to consider the alternative actions we're giving up. But just because you didn't notice a trade-off doesn't mean there wasn't one. In fact, many of our worst decisions come from ignoring opportunity costs. We all from time to time spend time, money, or effort on things we may later regret, while giving up things that we wish we had done instead.

This concept applies to public decisions too. When governments spend money on one thing, they can't spend it on something else. Every bridge, grant, or subsidy comes with an unseen cost. That cost is something else that didn't get funded. The broken window logic works the same way whether the window belongs to a baker or to an entire economy.

The Bottom Line

You pay for everything with something, even if that something is just time, energy, or the road not taken. Opportunity cost reminds us that trade-offs are everywhere. The visible cost is easy to spot. The invisible cost is what separates clear thinking from careless thinking. If you want to make better choices, don't just ask, "What am I getting?" Also ask, "What am I giving up?"

Chapter Eleven

We Decide One Step At A Time

One Takeaway

Most decisions aren't all or nothing, they're about what happens next. Thinking on the margin helps you make smarter, more flexible choices.

Life is Made Up of Steps

Most of life's decisions aren't grand, sweeping either/or moments. They're incremental. Do I eat another slice of pizza? Stay one more hour at the party? Work a little longer tonight? The way we make these choices—one step at a time—is what economists call **thinking on the margin.**

Marginal thinking is about the cost and benefit of one more unit of something. It doesn't ask, "Should I do this or not at all?" It asks, "Is doing this one more time worth it?"

This concept might seem small, but it has big implications.

More Isn't Always Better

Every decision involves trade-offs, but the value we get from each additional unit tends to shrink as we get more.

- The first slice of pizza is delicious.
- The second is still good.
- By the fifth, you might start to regret your choices.

Even though the slices are identical, the benefit you get from each one drops over time. This is why people stop eating when they're full and why most of us don't binge-watch TV forever, even when we love a show. The next unit brings less and less benefit.

How This Shapes Everyday Decisions

Marginal thinking is future-focused. It asks, "What will I gain from one more step, and what will it cost me?"

- **At work:** Is staying late worth the extra pay, or will it cost me sleep and family time?
- **In your budget:** Is spending this $20 now worth more than what it could become later?
- **In your schedule:** Does saying yes to one more commitment help you, or leave you burned out?

This framework helps you evaluate decisions based on where you are now, not where you've been.

You've Spent What You've Spent

Imagine you own an old car. You've already spent half your savings fixing the transmission. A week later, the radiator cracks. Do you fix it or walk away?

Marginal thinking says: what matters now is whether spending more will make you better off going forward.

1. Forget what you've already spent. The cost of the previous repair should not influence your choice; it's gone and can't be recovered (economists call this a **sunk cost**).

2. Instead, what matters now is whether spending the rest of your savings on this repair will make you better off going forward compared to other options, such as buying a different car.

Too often, we get stuck trying to justify past decisions. **But wise choices are made by looking forward, not backward.** Marginal thinking gives you permission to cut your losses and make the next best move.

Water, Diamonds, and the Value of Things

Here's a question that puzzled economists for almost a century. Water is essential to life. Diamonds are not. So why do diamonds cost so much more than water?

The answer is marginal thinking.

You're never choosing between all the water in the world and all the diamonds. If you were, you'd pick water in a heartbeat. But that's not the choice you face. You're choosing between one more glass of water and one more diamond.

Water is abundant. Your next glass probably isn't saving your life. It's watering a plant or filling a pot for pasta. The marginal value is low because you already have plenty.

Diamonds are scarce. The next one available still commands a high price because there aren't many of them relative to the people who want one.

The paradox disappears once you stop thinking about total importance and start thinking about what the next unit is worth. And that's how we actually make decisions. Not between everything and nothing, but between a little more and a little less.

The Bottom Line

We live life at the margins. By focusing on the next step, what it adds and what it costs, you can make smarter, more satisfying decisions. Marginal thinking keeps you anchored in reality. It helps you ignore sunk costs, avoid overdoing it, and focus on what matters right now.

Chapter Twelve

Short Answer: We Choose Based On What We Know

Your Coffee Shop Just Raised Its Prices

Your usual coffee shop just raised prices by a dollar. Your latte went from $5 to $6. You notice it on the menu board and feel a small flash of annoyance. Now what?

A month ago, you might have just paid it without thinking. Or, you may have switched shops out of frustration. But now you have a better way to work through this.

Start where it matters most. Before worrying about whether $6 is too much, ask a more basic question: is this place actually good? Does the coffee taste the way you want it to? Is the location convenient? Does it reliably get your order right? When you do this, you're checking for the effectiveness of what you're buying. You're doing this to make sure the thing works before optimizing how much you pay for it. If the shop isn't actually delivering what you value, the price doesn't matter. You should have left at $5.

Now look at what you're really giving up. The extra dollar doesn't sound like much. But you come here every workday. That's roughly $250 a year. What else could that money do? A few months of a streaming service. A nice dinner. A small step toward a savings goal. The dollar isn't just a dollar.

It's everything else that dollar could have been. When you do this you see the invisible cost right now, not just the price on the board.

Then think about this specific moment, not the general question. You're not deciding whether coffee is worth drinking for the rest of your life. You're deciding whether this cup, today, at this price, given everything else going on, is worth it. Maybe today it is. You're exhausted. You have a big meeting. You NEED this. Maybe tomorrow it isn't. You slept well. You have coffee at home. Your need is lower. The decision changes because your circumstances change.

You pay the $6. A few weeks later, you realize you've been coming three days a week instead of five. You didn't make a dramatic decision. You just started noticing the trade-off each time, and some mornings the situation pointed you toward the coffee at home.

That's what these tools do. They don't guarantee you'll always choose right. They make you deliberate about choices we can all make on autopilot. And when something doesn't work out, now you'll have a quick way to figure out why and what to adjust next time.

How Do Millions Of Strangers Cooperate?

Here's where economics gets fascinating. Somehow, millions of people making their own separate decisions manage to coordinate without anyone being in charge. How can this happen when no one is managing the system?

Chapter Thirteen

We Let Each Other Know What We Want

One Takeaway

Demand isn't a number. It's a reflection of what people value.

Your Wants Matter

What people want, and are willing to pay for, is one of the most important forces in economics. We call this **demand**, but it's really just a formal way of saying: **people act on what they value.**

Demand reflects purposeful, individual decisions. It's not a single number or a graph. It's what happens when real people weigh their options, compare trade-offs, and try to get more of what they want in life. Understanding demand starts with understanding people's wants and actions.

What Is Demand?

Demand describes the amount of a good or service that people are both willing and able to buy at different prices. It connects desire with action. Wanting something isn't enough. You need to want it and be in a position to purchase it.

But demand is more than the willingness to buy. It's shaped by:

- Preferences
- Circumstances
- Resources
- Expectations

What someone demands today may be very different from what they demanded yesterday, or will tomorrow.

Value Is Personal

The foundation of demand is **subjective value.** A good has no value in itself. Its worth depends on how well it helps someone achieve a specific goal in a specific moment.

- A bottle of water is almost worthless to someone walking past a dozen water fountains. It's priceless to someone stranded in the desert.
- A concert ticket might mean everything to a devoted fan and nothing to someone who's never heard the band before.

This is why demand is so dynamic, and why **no one can determine with certainty what people should want.**

The Law of Demand

As the price of a good goes up, people usually buy less of it. As the price falls, they tend to buy more. This is what is known as the law of demand. It's a fact of our world because people face trade-offs. Higher prices make people pause and ask, "Is this really worth it? Or should I hold off, buy less, or switch to something else?"

The key is we don't demand goods in isolation. We demand them relative to everything else we could be doing with our time or money.

Thinking on the Margin

Demand is shaped by marginal thinking. The value of that next unit of some good tends to go down when compared with the previous one. A great example is pizza. Each slice of pizza satisfies a less important hunger or want.

- The first slice hits the spot when you're really hungry. That's your most urgent need.
- The second slice is still tasty, but less necessary.
- By the third or fourth, you're starting to feel full.
- Eventually, another slice isn't just less satisfying. It might make you uncomfortable.

Each new unit of a good brings less satisfaction than the one before. **Since each new unit takes care of a less important want, your willingness to pay the same amount for each additional unit goes down.**

You might be willing to pay $4 for the first slice because you're starving. But you wouldn't pay $4 each for a second or third. If the price dropped to $2, maybe you'd go for two slices. If it dropped to $1.50, maybe three. As the price falls, you become more willing to take care of those less urgent wants, so your quantity demanded increases.

What Influences Demand?

People's willingness to buy something depends on more than price. A few important factors include:

- **Income**: More income expands options and can change preferences.
- **Substitutes**: If coffee becomes too expensive, you might switch to tea.
- **Complements**: If gas prices go up, demand for gas-guzzling cars might fall.
- **Expectations**: If you think prices will eventually rise, you might buy more now.
- **Trends and Tastes**: Fashions change, and so do desires.
- **Population**: More people = more potential demand.

These aren't static. They change constantly, which means demand is always evolving.

Demand as a Signal

When lots of people value a good and are willing to pay for it, that demand sends a signal. It tells producers: make more of this. When demand falls, it sends a different message: do something else.

Demand doesn't just reflect what people want. It directs resources toward what they value most.

The Bottom Line

Demand reflects our needs, preferences, and goals in real time. It helps guide production, signal scarcity, and align resources with value. And since people are always changing, so is demand.

Chapter Fourteen

We (Try To) Make What Other People Want

One Takeaway

Supply reflects how producers respond to incentives, manage trade-offs, and adapt to what people value.

What Is Supply?

Supply refers to the quantity of a good or service that people are willing and able to spend their time and money to produce and offer for sale at different prices. It's how producers respond to the needs and wants of others, but not out of charity. They do it because it makes sense for them to.

Producers take action when they believe there is an opportunity where others place a higher value on something that is greater than the producer's (expected) cost to make it. When the payoff is worth it, producers figure out how to create, build, or provide something. When it's not, they stop.

Supply isn't fixed. It shifts based on costs, technology, policy, and competition. But at its core, it's a reflection of people trying to meet the needs of others in ways that also benefit themselves.

The Law of Supply: Why Prices Matter

As prices rise, producers are generally more willing to supply more of a good. Why? Because higher prices:

- Help cover the rising costs of producing more.
- Attract new sellers who now see an opportunity to profit.
- Signal that buyers place a higher value on the good.

Think of a local bakery. If cupcakes are selling for $3 each, it might make sense to bake 100 a day. But if the price jumps to $6? It might be worth hiring extra help to make 150. **The higher price makes more effort and resources worthwhile.**

Costs and Trade-Offs

Producers face the same basic limit we all do: they can't do everything at once. They must choose how to use their time, tools, labor, and materials. Every decision to make one thing means not making something else.

For example:

- A farmer can plant wheat or soybeans, not both, on the same land.
- A factory can assemble bicycles or scooters, but not all day, every day.

These trade-offs, or opportunity costs, shape supply decisions.

Marginal Thinking in Supply

Just like consumers, producers think on the margin. They ask: Is making one more unit worth it?

Let's say:

- A factory produces 1,000 shirts per day without issue.
- Producing 1,500 might require extra shifts or new machines.

The first few extra shirts might be profitable. But if each new shirt costs more than it brings in, it's time to stop. Marginal costs eventually rise, which puts a limit on supply.

What Shapes Supply?

Several factors influence how much gets made:

- **Input Costs:** If raw materials or labor costs go up, supply may shrink.
- **Technology:** Better tools and methods can lower costs and expand supply.
- **Regulation and Taxes:** Rules that increase costs make some production less worthwhile.
- **Expectations:** If producers expect demand to rise soon, they may scale up now.
- **Competition:** More sellers or producers generally increases overall supply.

Supply is a Process

Supply is not just a number, it's a process. It's a constant adjustment in response to consumer demand, costs, and limits. **The best producers are those who adapt, shift, and evolve.** They're not just making things; they're trying to make what people want, before someone else does.

The Bottom Line

Supply reflects how people make decisions to serve others—so long as it serves them too. It's shaped by prices, costs, and trade-offs. Behind every good you see for sale is someone who believed it was worth the effort to produce. Understanding supply helps explain how our economy adjusts to change, meets new needs, and continues to grow.

Chapter Fifteen

We Don't Set Prices, We Discover Them

One Takeaway

Prices are signals, not just random numbers. They coordinate billions of decisions and help us adapt, cooperate, and thrive without anyone needing to be in charge.

What Is The Price System?

Prices might be humanity's most powerful coordination technology. The thing is, they're often misunderstood.

Prices come from the everyday decisions of buyers and sellers, each acting on their own knowledge, values, and limits. Prices are discovered through things like negotiation, trade, and interaction.

But, they do far more than tell us what something costs.

Prices share information. They help us choose what to produce, how much to buy, and when to change course. They reflect both the value people place on things and the scarcity of the resources needed to make them.

What Prices Actually Do

At a glance, prices might look like a tag on a shelf or a line on a receipt. But underneath, they're doing serious work:

- **They help people plan.** Businesses use prices to compare options, estimate potential demand, and decide whether something is worth producing.

- **They guide behavior.** A rising price says, "People want more of this," encouraging others to step in and supply it.

- **They respond in real time.** If an avocado shortage hits, prices rise. That signals consumers to buy less and producers to ship more.

- **They bundle knowledge.** A price reflects everything from weather patterns to labor shortages—even if you don't know it. You don't need to read a global supply chain report to know oranges are more expensive this year. The price already tells you.

All this happens without anyone needing full information.

Prices and Social Cooperation

One of the great miracles of our world is that millions of strangers can coordinate without speaking a word.

You can sip coffee grown in Guatemala, sweetened with sugar from Brazil, poured into a mug made in Ohio, and never once meet the people who made it possible. Prices link your life with theirs. They align actions across borders and time zones. You don't need to know how to grow beans or refine sugar. The price tells you what it's worth to others and what it will cost you to enjoy it.

When We Get in the Way

Prices work best when they're free to change as needed. But when they're held down or pushed up, usually by laws or policies, the entire feedback loop can break.

Imagine a bakery. Flour prices go up due to a drought. That single change ripples through the price system. The baker might raise prices, reduce output, or switch to recipes using less flour. Customers may respond by buying fewer baked goods or switching to something else entirely.

Now imagine the government steps in and says flour can't cost more than it used to. The information and signals vanish. The baker doesn't cut back. Flour runs out. Shelves stay empty. Everyone's frustrated, even though the decision was made with good intentions.

Specific Examples

- **Rent controls** might make housing cheaper for some, but they can lead to shortages, neglect, or disrepair.

- **Minimum wages** might help some workers, but can unintentionally price others out of a job if businesses can't afford to hire at the mandated level.

- **Subsidies from government spending** might make prices lower for a bit, but they distort demand. When something feels artificially cheap, people use more of it—whether or not that's the best use of resources.

None of these negative outcomes happen because people involved in these situations are bad actors. It's because signals can get scrambled by well-meaning policies.

In each case people think they're acting on good information, but instead they're acting on information that's unintentionally not reflecting reality.

Why Relying on Prices Works Better Than Planning

No one, not even the smartest policymaker, can gather and process all the information embedded in every price. Attempts to do so will almost always fall short. Why? Because the simple fact is no one can have access to all the real-time knowledge of every person's wants, values, trade-offs, and priorities. But prices do.

The Bottom Line

The price system is a tool used for coordination, built from the choices of millions. When we let them do their job, we unlock cooperation at a scale no planner could ever copy. The result isn't just efficiency. It's resilience, adaptability, and the freedom to act on what matters most to each of us.

Chapter Sixteen

We Pay For Value Not Effort

One Takeaway

Costs don't determine prices. Consumers' willingness to pay does. Value flows from the consumer backward to producers and guides what gets made and how.

Who Really Sets Prices?

It feels intuitive to think that prices are simply a business' costs added up with a profit margin tacked onto the top. That may be how some management books help business owners get the ball rolling with their company in the short run, but it's not how the economy actually works in the long run. And it doesn't reflect the main mission of every business: meeting the needs of consumers.

In reality, **consumers dictate prices.** Or more precisely, the price reflects what consumers are willing to pay.

If buyers don't think something is worth the asking price, it doesn't sell; no matter how much it costs to produce.

For example, a coffee shop can't charge $10 for a cup just because the beans were expensive from a limited small batch. If customers aren't willing to pay that much, the shop must either lower the price, improve the experience, or go out of business. The consumer has the final say.

Price Comes Before Cost

It might feel backwards, but value flows from the customer to the business, not the other way around. Here's how it works:

- **Customers express what they value** by what they're willing to pay and actually making a purchase.
- **Producers adjust their budgets, inputs, and strategies** to meet those preferences.
- **Resources (like labor, materials, and tools)** get their value from how much they help create things consumers want and from producers competing to buy them.

Think about smartphones. If consumers start buying based on camera features, phone makers will bid more for the sensors and chips needed to deliver the best experience. Those components didn't become valuable on their own. They became valuable because consumers wanted the results they helped create.

How Are Costs Determined?

Costs come from competition. Every producer is trying to buy the same limited pool of resources. These resources can include things like skilled labor, land, equipment, or ingredients. **The more valuable a resource is in creating something producers believe people want, the more producers will be willing to pay for it.**

Take microchips. If automakers and smartphone manufacturers are both racing to buy them, prices may rise. But those prices are just a reflection of that input's ability to create what consumers want. Producers don't just buy inputs. They bid for the ability to meet consumer demand using those inputs.

What This Means for Businesses

If you're producing something, your job isn't to justify your costs. It's to create something people are willing to pay for.

Focus on customer value first. You don't get to decide what your product is worth. Your customers do. **Work backwards.** Start from what people want, then figure out what you can afford to spend to deliver it. **Don't confuse effort with value.** A diamond found on the beach is worth the same to a buyer as one mined by a team of 12. The consumer doesn't pay for your struggle. They pay for what it means to them.

Why This Matters

This idea has real consequences for how resources are used and how businesses succeed or fail.

A producer who ignores what customers want will likely overspend and underdeliver. A business that listens carefully to what consumers want can find creative, efficient ways to meet demand. Transactions, driven by consumer choice, reward how well producers respond to consumers.

This simple fact also keeps everyone honest. No one can just raise prices and force someone to cover their mistakes. If the consumers don't want a product or service, it doesn't sell.

The Bottom Line

Consumers don't care what something costs you. They care what it's worth to them. And that simple truth keeps the economy focused on what matters most: creating real value for real people.

Chapter Seventeen

We Make Order Without Orders

One Takeaway

Order often doesn't require control. Instead, order requires people to be able to pursue their goals, respond to prices, and adjust to others.

We Don't Need a Master Plan

Think about your last cup of coffee. Did someone carefully design every step? Was there some overseer planting the beans, roasting them, shipping them, and stocking the shelves, all just for you?

Of course not. And yet, somehow, it all came together. That's the power of **spontaneous order**: an outcome that looks planned but isn't. It happens not because someone is in charge, but because individuals (each with their own goals) cooperate through markets without even realizing it.

No one needs to know the entire process. A coffee farmer doesn't know who you are. The barista doesn't know who harvested the beans. But each person in that chain does their part because they see an opportunity to benefit. The result is your morning caffeine fix.

What Is Spontaneous Order?

Spontaneous order is what happens when

- **People act in their own interest.**
- **Prices guide behavior.**
- **Exchange brings people together.**

Without needing top-down direction, people adapt, experiment, and respond to what others do. Through trial and error (and the price system) we get what feels like magic. People work together and solve incredibly complex problems without someone overseeing everything.

When it comes to your morning coffee, the farmer grows beans to earn a living, not as a personal favor to you. The shipping company responds to rising demand by adjusting routes and prices. And finally, you buy a bag of beans or a cup of coffee because it smells great and fits your budget.

Nobody sees the whole system. Yet everyone contributes to its success.

Why Spontaneous Order Matters

Spontaneous order scales. No one person could manage the decisions needed to supply coffee (or anything else) to millions of people every day. Spontaneous order handles complexity far better than a room full of experts ever could.

It adapts. Markets (the combined actions taken by millions of individuals every day) shift when something changes. This can be for any number of reasons such as a drought in Brazil or a new flavor trend in Los Angeles. The system adjusts without anyone needing permission to make a change.

It surprises us. Some of the most powerful innovations—like language or even the internet—weren't designed from the top down. They evolved from the bottom up, through trial, error, and cooperation.

An Example

Take the global supply chain for a smartphone. Rare earth minerals from Africa. Computer chips from Taiwan. Screens from South Korea. Assembly in China. Logistics by air, sea, and truck. Millions of decisions made by people who don't know each other and likely never speak to each other. And yet, somehow the phone arrives in your pocket.

This kind of order can't be built by blueprint. It emerges from incentives, signals, and voluntary choices.

Why It Works in More Than Just Markets

Spontaneous order can apply to all social behavior. You can find it in organizations, teams, even communities. When people are given the freedom to respond to available knowledge, you get:

- **More innovation.** People closest to the problem find the best solutions.
- **More ownership.** When people shape the systems they use, they care more.
- **More agility.** Things move faster when decisions don't require constant approval.

Good managers in organizations know when to guide and when to get out of the way. They recognize the benefits of spontaneous order even if they don't know what to call it.

Planned vs. Unplanned

Planning isn't always bad. For simple, repeatable tasks, it can be powerful and necessary. **But the more complex and dynamic the system, the more you should trust in spontaneous order.** Rigid plans can't keep up with real-time information, shifting preferences, or unpredictable events.

Markets solve these challenges not through control, but through countless small, individual adjustments made by regular people acting on what they know and what they want.

The Bottom Line

The economy is a living process. It is messy, creative, adaptive, and out of any one person's control. Because of this it produces unintended benefits. When people are free to go after their goals, respond to price signals, and trade with one another, remarkable things happen. Not because anyone planned it, but because no one had to.

Chapter Eighteen

Short Answer: We Send Signals With Our Purchases

How Your Coffee Got Here Without Anyone Planning It

Let's go back to your morning coffee and look at it from a new angle. Not about your decision to buy it, but how it got to the counter in the first place.

Someone grew these beans. Someone who probably lived thousands of miles away. Someone else bought them, shipped them across an ocean, roasted them, and delivered them to a shop in your neighborhood. Dozens of strangers worked together across continents to put this exact cup in your hand at a price you were willing to pay.

Nobody planned it. There's no Coffee Coordination Committee deciding how many beans to grow, which roast to produce, or where to ship the result. It happened because you and millions of other people sent a signal every time you bought a cup: "I value this enough to pay for it."

That signal traveled. The shop owner saw that medium roast outsold dark roast, so she adjusted her orders. The roaster saw the shift and bid more for the right beans. A farmer in Colombia saw better prices being offered to buy specific varieties and planted more of them. Your preference reshaped someone's livelihood on another continent...and neither of you has any idea the other exists.

And this coordination isn't just happening across oceans. Look at the block where your coffee shop sits. There's probably a bakery nearby. Maybe a dry cleaner or a daycare. Nobody assigned those businesses to those locations. But each one makes the others more valuable. The parent drops off the child, grabs coffee and a pastry, picks up dry cleaning on the way home. That clustering emerged because each owner followed their own signals about where customers were and what they needed. Order, without anyone giving orders.

Now here's what makes this useful beyond a fun fact about coffee.

Once you see this coordination happening in your cup, you start seeing it everywhere. Seeing this can change how you evaluate almost everything.

When someone says a product is "overpriced," you'll think about what the price is actually telling you. Maybe it reflects a drought in a growing region, or rising shipping costs, or the fact that a lot of other people want the same thing. The price isn't arbitrary. It's carrying information from thousands of people you'll never meet.

When someone proposes controlling a price — capping rent, setting a minimum wage, subsidizing a product — you'll ask what signal that overrides. If a price is a message, what happens when you force a different message? Who adjusts their behavior, and how?

When a new product appears that you didn't know you wanted, you'll recognize the process that created it. Someone, somewhere, noticed a signal. They saw an unmet need, a shifting preference, or a gap between what people valued and what was available. Then they acted on it.

Your morning coffee isn't just a drink. It's a window into how the world organizes itself without anyone being in charge. And now that you can see through that window, you'll notice coordination, and its absence, in places most people never think to look.

What Makes Cooperation So Valuable?

Strangers use prices and signals to work together. This coordination transforms our differences into opportunities for mutual gain. The fact that we want different things, have different skills, and live in different places isn't a problem that needs solving. It's a foundation of growth. To understand why cooperation creates so much value, we need to look deeper into how people actually work together.

Chapter Nineteen

We Discover Through Trade

One Takeaway

Markets work because people are always experimenting. Profits and losses help us learn what works and, importantly, what doesn't.

What Is the Market?

When people talk about "the market," it can sound like a place, a machine, or maybe even some thinking and scheming force of nature. But the market isn't a machine. It's a **process** made up of people trying, learning, adjusting, and exchanging in real time.

Markets are what happen when individuals pursue their own goals, make plans, and interact with others through voluntary exchange. From these separate actions, we get coordination, innovation, and progress. Not because someone designed it that way, but because people respond to signals, incentives, and feedback.

Discovery in Action

A few decades ago, almost nobody would have paid for a bottle of water.

Tap water was free, clean, and pretty much everywhere. Then someone tried selling it anyway. Some people laughed. But others bought it. They started selling it at the gym, at the airport, on a hot day when convenience mattered more than cost.

That experiment revealed something no survey or study could have predicted: people would pay for water when the context was right. Other entrepreneurs noticed. Flavored water appeared. Sparkling water followed. Electrolyte water. Alkaline water. Each one was another experiment. Some succeeded. Some quietly disappeared from shelves. The ones that stuck weren't planned by anyone. They were discovered through millions of small transactions, each one sending a signal about what people actually valued.

Nobody sat down and designed the bottled water industry. It emerged because one person tried something, the market responded, and others learned from that response. That's what discovery looks like.

How Markets Work

The market process is a cycle of communication, action, and adjustment:

- **Consumers communicate** what they want by spending their money.

- **Producers respond** by creating goods and services they think will meet those wants.

- **Entrepreneurs experiment** and try new ideas, business models, or products in hopes of turning a profit.

- **Prices for goods and services go up and down** as conditions change, guiding people toward better uses of their time and resources.

No central expert tells millions of people what to do, but through prices and profit-and-loss, the market process coordinates their actions anyway.

Why It's a Process, Not a Blueprint

The market is dynamic, not fixed. It isn't perfect, but it doesn't have to be. It works precisely because it doesn't expect perfection.

People make mistakes. Businesses fail. Plans fall apart. But every mistake is information. Every loss is a signal. When something doesn't work, producers adapt. When something does work, others may notice, copy, and maybe improve it. That's how markets learn.

Profit tells us when resources are being used in a way that people value.

Loss tells us when they're not.

This trial-and-error process is what makes markets so powerful. They're not designed by experts to work perfectly. They evolve from trial and error and reward continued improvement.

Markets Reflect Human Action

The market process is so effective because it's built around human action.

- **We all want different things.**
- **We all have different skills.**
- **We all face different limits.**

Markets allow each of us to act on our own knowledge and preferences, and find a way to cooperate without being told how.

This means the market doesn't need one person, or even one group, to be "in charge." The coordination emerges from millions of decisions made by ordinary people. Each person contributes a piece of the puzzle. **Prices, profit, and loss are the signals that help those pieces fit together.**

The Bottom Line

The market is not a machine. It's a process based on trial, error, profit, and loss. People don't just trade goods and services. They trade ideas, experiments, feedback, and wants. And through that, we learn. It's how we figure out what works, and what's worth doing better.

(On a personal note, my mother insists that she came up with the idea of bottled water when she was 12 years old, at a picnic in Las Vegas long before anyone else. Like the old saying goes, necessity is the mother of invention, and the Las Vegas heat definitely makes water a necessity. I don't know about you, but boiling water from an outdoor hose isn't the greatest thirst quencher. She may have seen the opportunity before anyone else. But, that's the thing about markets. Having the idea isn't the discovery. The discovery happens when someone tries to make it. Someone else pays for it. And everyone learns something they didn't know before.)

Chapter Twenty

We Can Do Anything, But We Can't Do Everything

One Takeaway

Focusing on what we do best lets us do less and achieve more, because no one can be good at everything, but together we can create almost anything.

Why Can't We Just Do Everything Ourselves?

Imagine if you had to grow your own food, make your own clothes, build your own house, and generate your own electricity. Life would be exhausting—and short. Luckily, we don't live in that world. We live in a world of **specialization**, where each of us does a few things really well and trades for the rest.

Specialization is what makes high living standards, innovation, and cooperating with others around the world possible. And it all starts with a simple reality: we each have limited time, energy, resources, and knowledge.

The Power of Specialization

Specialization happens when people focus on doing one type of work. This allows them to build expertise, learn to make less mistakes, and produce more than they personally need. From there, trade naturally follows.

- A baker bakes bread not just to feed themselves, but for others to eat too.
- A carpenter makes furniture not just for their home, but for customers' homes too.
- A software engineer writes code not to solve every problem in their life, but to serve millions of users.

Each of these people depends on others for their food, housing, transportation, clothing, and tools. And yet, they're better off than if they tried to do it all themselves.

Why Dividing Labor Works

Breaking big tasks into smaller roles, which economists call the **division of labor**, allows groups, companies, and societies to grow far beyond what any individual could achieve alone.

This works because:

- **Repetition builds skill.** Doing one task over and over leads to mastery.
- **Time is used more efficiently.** Less switching between tasks means more focus.
- **Trade connects people.** Everyone can rely on others for what they don't produce.

Whether you're on a factory line, a film crew, or a startup team, dividing tasks and trusting others to do their part gets better results in less time.

The Dinner Party Principle

Picture three friends cooking dinner. If everyone tries to do everything—chop, stir, sauté, plate—it's chaos. But if one chops, another cooks, and the third sets the table, dinner is ready fast and (hopefully) stress-free.

Now imagine this scaled up to a city, a country, or the world. The same principle holds: **millions of people do the work they do best, and trust others to do the rest.** That's how airplanes are built, hospitals run, and your morning coffee ends up in your hand.

More Than Just Productivity

Specialization without a doubt boosts output. But in doing so, it improves quality of life. It leads to:

- **Higher living standards:** We get access to better goods at lower costs.

- **More time for leisure:** Productivity frees up time for rest, play, and learning.

- **More opportunity:** By trading what we do best, we can earn more and reach more people.

It's not about doing everything. It's about doing **the right things** and letting others do theirs.

The Bottom Line

We thrive by doing what we do best and trading with others for

the rest. Specialization and the division of labor unlock more wealth, more growth, and more cooperation. These ideas allow individuals to live better lives by doing less, not more. They also lead to increasing trust that someone, somewhere, is willing to fill in the gaps of what else we need.

Chapter Twenty-One

We Are Best Off When We All Play To Our Strengths

One Takeaway

Even if you're great at everything, you're better off focusing on what you do best, and letting others do the rest.

Why Not Just Do It All Yourself?

You may be the most capable person on your team, in your family, or at your company. But being the best at everything doesn't mean you should do everything. Economists call this idea **comparative advantage**.

It's one of the most powerful ideas in economics. It's all about how we work with each other. Comparative advantage shows that even if one person is better at everything, two people working together can still achieve more by focusing on what each does *relatively* better.

A Simple Example

Imagine you and your kid are tackling two garden tasks: **pulling weeds** and **planting rose bushes.** Neither of you wants to spend more time than necessary on these chores. You're faster at both. But, that doesn't mean you should do both.

Let's say you can pull 25 weeds in the same time it takes your kid to pull 12. You also can plant 5 rose bushes in the same time your kid plants 4.

Task	You (per hour)	Your Kid (per hour)
Pull Weeds	25	12
Plant Roses	5	4

If you spend one hour planting roses, you give up the chance to pull 25 weeds. Your kid only gives up 12 weeds in the same situation. That's a smaller sacrifice. So, while you're better at both tasks, it costs you more (in terms of weeds) to plant roses than it costs your kid.

This means your time is relatively better spent pulling weeds, and your kid's time is relatively better spent planting roses. **If each of you specializes based on comparative advantage and then cooperates, you get more chores done in the same amount of time.**

Why It Works

Comparative advantage isn't about being the best. It's about **what you give up** when you choose to do one task instead of another (your opportunity cost). If your opportunity cost is higher, it makes sense to let someone else take the lead. This is true even if you're faster.

This idea shows up everywhere.

A CEO may have a knack for graphic design, but they'll likely create more value focusing on strategy and hiring others to design.

A brilliant surgeon could also be a good administrator, but they save more lives by spending time in the operating room and hiring an office manager.

Even someone less skilled overall still has something valuable to contribute when they focus on where their trade-offs are smallest.

The Big Idea Behind Cooperation

Comparative advantage is one of the secrets behind why trade is so beneficial. If we all tried to do everything ourselves, we'd be less productive, more stressed, and far less wealthy. Instead:

- **We specialize in what we're relatively good at.**
- **We exchange what we produce for what others produce.**
- **We all end up better off—even if some of us could do both jobs on our own.**

In short, we create more value together than we ever could alone.

The Bottom Line

You don't have to be the best at everything to be valuable, and trying to do it all yourself is usually a bad idea. Comparative advantage shows us that productivity and progress come from smart trade-offs, focused effort, and mutual work. We do better by doing less—together.

Chapter Twenty-Two

We Trade Because We See Value Differently

One Takeaway

Voluntary exchange works because people value things differently. Those differences create opportunities for everyone to be better off.

What Makes a Trade Worth It?

When you freely hand over $10 for a sandwich you are saying that in that moment, you value the sandwich more than the $10 in your pocket. And the person behind the counter? They value the $10 more than the sandwich they just made. You both walk away feeling like you got the better deal.

That's the magic of **voluntary exchange.** It's not a win-lose scenario. It's a **win-win.** Both sides willingly agree to trade based on their own judgment of what's worth more to them. **If both believe they are better off, then both win.**

This idea isn't just for sandwiches and $10 bills. It's the foundation of how people cooperate, specialize, and build wealth together.

Why Trade Benefits Both Parties

To an outsider, some trades might look unfair. Maybe you sold an old television for $50 that once cost you $300. Or someone swapped a rare collectible for less cash than you'd expect. But here's the thing: *value is personal.* **If both people said "yes" to the trade, that means both expected to gain something from it.**

Nobody is forced. Nobody is tricked. Both sides act on what matters most to them at the time. Even if someone later regrets the trade, that doesn't mean the trade was unjust. It means people sometimes learn after the fact.

In economics, we don't judge trades based on hindsight. We focus on the moment of choice, where each person believes they're better off.

Why Trade Creates Wealth (Even Without Making More Stuff)

Voluntary trade doesn't always create new goods, but it *does* create more value. That's because:

- It moves goods into the hands of those who value them most.
- It frees people to specialize and focus on what they do best.
- It turns competition into cooperation, aligning incentives.

A farmer with extra vegetables can trade for carpentry. A musician can trade a performance for equipment repairs. **Each person gets more value from the trade than they could create on their own.**

A Simple Example: The Garage Sale

Imagine selling a dusty old bike at your garage sale for $100. To you, it's just taking up space. To the buyer, it's a sweet deal and a new ride. You each gain something you value more than what you gave up. No new bike was built, but both of you are better off than before the trade.

That's wealth creation through voluntary exchange.

The (Good) Salesperson's Secret

Good salespeople understand that trade isn't about persuasion. It's about value alignment.

A smart seller doesn't try to convince you that an item is "worth" something in the abstract. They ask what you care about, and then show how the product meets *your* needs.

When buyers and sellers understand each other's goals, they can make deals where both walk away happy.

Why It Matters

Voluntary exchange is how people cooperate without needing to agree on everything. You don't need to like what someone else likes. You just need to want what they're offering more than what you're giving up. That simple truth powers economies, builds businesses, and helps people solve problems together.

The Bottom Line

Every voluntary trade is a quiet act of cooperation. It's how we align different values to create mutual gain. We don't need to force anyone. We just need to listen, offer, and agree. And when that happens, everyone walks away better off. Even if they value things differently.

Chapter Twenty-Three

We Use Money Because We Both Want It

One Takeaway

Money makes trade possible, but it isn't wealth. Money is a tool that helps us exchange what we've created for what others have made.

What is Money, Really?

Money touches nearly every part of our lives, yet few people stop to ask: What is money? At its core, money is just a tool. It's a commonly accepted **medium of exchange.** It allows us to trade easily, efficiently, and with nearly everyone else.

Without money, every transaction would require a direct swap: "I'll give you this if you give me that." Direct swaps like this are called **barter.** While barter can work in small, simple communities, it breaks down quickly in more complex settings.

Why Barter Breaks Down

Imagine you're a dairy farmer and need eggs. Your neighbor raises chickens, but they don't want milk. They want oranges. Now you have to find someone with oranges who also wants milk. This is called the **double coincidence of wants**, and it's incredibly inefficient. It would be better if both of you always had what the other wanted.

Money solves this problem. You sell your milk for money and then use that money to buy eggs. Everyone can now trade more easily, even if they don't directly want what the other person spends their life making. **That's what makes money powerful: it connects people with different needs in a seamless, scalable way.**

What Makes Something "Good" Money?

Not everything can function as money. To be widely accepted, a good form of money should be:

- **Uniform**: One unit should be the same as any other.
- **Portable**: Easy to carry and transfer.
- **Divisible**: You can split it into smaller units without losing value.
- **Recognizable**: People can easily identify and trust it.
- **Durable**: It doesn't wear out quickly.
- **Hard to Fake**: It needs to be difficult to counterfeit.

Historically, gold, silver, and even shells have served this role. Today, we use government-issued currency.

Money Isn't Wealth—It's a Claim on Wealth

Money itself doesn't feed you, house you, or keep you warm. It's not valuable because of what it *is*, but because of what it *lets you do*. Money is a claim on real goods and services that other people have produced that you can now access through trade.

This is why the world can't print its way to prosperity. **More dollars don't mean there's magically more goods to satisfy people's wants.** If everyone suddenly had twice as much money, but the number of homes, clothes, and food stayed the same, prices would just rise to meet the new money supply. You'd be no better off. You'd have more zeroes in your bank account, but the same pounds of beef in your freezer.

Why Stability Matters

A stable money supply allows people to save, plan, and invest with confidence. When governments or central banks alter or influence the value of money by printing too much of it, or by pushing interest rates too high or low, they can distort the signals that guide our decisions. These distortions can lead to wasted resources, failed investments, and long-term harm to the economy.

Money is like a measuring stick. If it keeps changing length, no one can build anything that lasts. And **money is like language.** If the meaning of words changes constantly, communication falls apart.

The same is true for trade and production.

A Final Thought on Money

Most economic activity today depends on the reliability of money. It enables everything from grocery shopping to international trade. But it's easy to forget: money works only because people trust it, and because it's tied to the value people create.

Printing more doesn't make us richer. Producing more things people want to trade for is what actually builds wealth.

The Bottom Line

Money is one of the greatest tools for human cooperation ever invented. It lets us trade without needing to barter, save without wasting, and coordinate without confusion. But it only works when it's stable and trusted. Remember: **money is a claim on value—not value itself.** True wealth comes not from printing more, but from creating more of what other people value.

Chapter Twenty-Four

Short Answer: We Turn Differences Into Opportunities

Why Your Coffee Exists at All

You've seen your morning coffee as a personal choice. You've seen it as a supply chain coordinated by signals. Now look at it one more time and ask why any of it is possible in the first place.

Your coffee exists because people are different. And those differences drive our economy.

The farmer in Colombia grows coffee because his climate, soil, and expertise give him an advantage at growing beans that you could never replicate in your backyard. He could try roasting his own coffee too, but he's relatively better at farming. So, he focuses on what he does best and trades the result.

The roaster in Portland has never set foot on a coffee farm. But she knows flavor profiles, roast timing, and how to bring out the best in a particular bean. She doesn't grow. She transforms. And she's better at that than almost anything else she could do with her time.

The barista at your shop can't roast and doesn't farm. But she knows her regulars, pulls a consistent shot, and creates an experience that keeps you coming back. Her specialization is the last link in a chain that stretches thousands of miles.

None of them could do what the others do as well as the others do it. That's not a problem. It's the engine. Each person focuses on their comparative advantage and trades the result. Everyone ends up with better coffee than any of them could produce alone.

And here's something easy to overlook: the trade only happens because each person values what they're getting more than what they're giving up. The farmer values your money more than the beans he's shipping. The roaster values the farmer's beans more than the cash she's paying. You value the latte more than the $6 in your pocket. Every link in this chain is held together by people seeing value differently. Each difference creates an opportunity for exchange that makes both sides better off.

Money is what makes all of this seamless. Without it, the farmer would need to find a roaster who happens to want raw beans and happens to have something the farmer wants in return. The roaster would need to barter directly with every shop she supplies. You'd need to offer your specific skills to the barista in exchange for a cup. Money lets everyone in this chain trade with everyone else without those impossible coincidences. It turned a web of differences into a forty-five second transaction at the register.

Here's the useful takeaway: most people assume that cooperation requires similarity. That the only way to cooperate is to have shared goals, shared values, shared priorities. Your coffee proves we don't have to agree or be the same on everything. Every person in that chain had different skills, different knowledge, and different values. That's not what they had to overcome to cooperate. That's what made cooperation worth doing in the first place.

The most valuable thing you can do — in business, in your community, in your relationships — isn't to make everyone the same. It's to find the differences and build on them. Your coffee is proof that this works.

Why Can't We Just Get Rich Quick?

We now know how important cooperation is to creating wealth. If it's that easy then why do some societies prosper while others struggle? Why does it feel like building wealth takes so long? Can't we just force everyone to cooperate and skip ahead to being rich? The answer lies in understanding what real growth actually requires and that there are no shortcuts.

Chapter Twenty-Five

We Grow By Producing, Not Just Consuming

One Takeaway

Long-term prosperity begins with production, not consumption. Nothing can be consumed that wasn't first produced by you or by someone else.

Someone Creates What We Consume

It's common to hear people say that spending drives the economy. You'll hear that "consumption makes up 70% of GDP," or that economic growth depends on getting people to spend more. This is true, but it flips the order of things. No one can consume what hasn't first been produced either by themselves or by someone else. You can't grow an economy by focusing only on spending.

Behind every sandwich, car, or concert ticket is one thing: production. Someone created something valuable. Only then can they, or someone else, consume it.

Production Comes First

Production means using resources (time, effort, tools, materials) to make something that others want. Whether it's plucking an apple from a tree, designing a smartphone, or teaching a class, production is what makes consumption possible.

Even in simple societies, no one can eat unless they first gather, hunt, or grow. Nothing gets consumed unless someone first creates, collects, or contributes something. In that sense, every act of consumption depends on someone's past act of production.

Consumption Is Good, But It's Not the Only Goal

Consumption satisfies our wants and needs in the short run. But if we consume everything we produce, there's nothing left to invest in tools, skills, or systems that help us produce more in the future. In this case, growth slows and options shrink.

Think of it like this: if a farmer eats all the grain they harvest and saves none to plant next season, their future harvest disappears.

What really fuels economic growth is the ability and willingness to:

- **Save some resources** rather than consume them all.
- **Invest those savings** into productive tools and processes.
- **Build capital goods**, like machines, that make future production easier and more efficient.

This shift, focusing less on consumer goods and more on capital goods, can transform living standards over time.

An Everyday Example

Take two communities. In the first, people work hard and spend everything they earn. In the second, people still enjoy life, but they also save a portion of their income and use it to invest in better tools, education, and infrastructure.

After a few years, the second community:

- Produces more with less effort
- Has higher wealth
- Offers more job opportunities and
- Enjoys greater stability

Why? Because they didn't just work and spend. They produced and reinvested.

Time Preferences: Now vs. Later

One of the key drivers behind all of this is what economists call **time preference**: how much you value things now versus in the future.

- **High time preference** means spending now, focusing on short-term enjoyment.
- **Low time preference** means delaying gratification and saving today so you can build something better for tomorrow.

Individuals with lower time preferences tend to invest, build skills, and grow businesses. Societies with lower time preferences tend to develop stronger economies.

Consumption Isn't Bad, but It's Not Enough

None of this means consumption is bad. It's necessary to live. It can also be the reward for productive effort, and it leads an enjoyable life. The simple point is, consumption is not the cause of growth. If we focus only on what people want today, we miss the chance to build a better tomorrow.

All work and no play isn't the goal. But all play and no work isn't either.

The Bottom Line

Economic growth is built on production. Creating, saving, and investing are what lay the groundwork for future prosperity. It's true in households, businesses, and entire economies. When we focus on producing and saving value, rather than just consuming it, we become able to build the tools, skills, and systems that make life better for everyone.

Chapter Twenty-Six

We Produce Now To Consume Later

One Takeaway

The more time and steps we invest in creating value, the more productive and prosperous we can become. If we're willing to wait.

Why Can't We Magically Have All We Want?

It's easy to take finished goods for granted. A sandwich. A car. A smartphone. But behind every product you consume is a long chain of choices, tools, and steps that took place before you ever saw it. Production isn't a straight line. It's a complex web that takes time to fully come together.

Some economists call this the **structure of production**. And while it might sound abstract, it's central to understanding how the economy works and why building wealth requires patience and planning.

From Raw Materials to Reality

Not all goods are the same. Some are made to be consumed immediately (like food or clothing). Others exist to help create those consumables (like tractors, factory equipment, or software systems). Economists refer to these as:

- **Lower-order goods**: Consumer goods used directly (like meals or phones).
- **Higher-order goods**: Capital goods and raw materials used to produce something else (like machines or lumber).

The more complex and productive an economy becomes, the more layers of higher-order goods exist behind the scenes. Your morning coffee requires beans, roasting equipment, packaging machinery, transportation trucks, and retail systems. Each step in the chain builds toward that brewed cup.

Roundabout Isn't a Detour

Production can work in **roundabout** ways. That might sound inefficient, but it's actually a strength. Taking the long way, by building tools or infrastructure first, can make future production easier, faster, and better.

Imagine two paths across a city:

- One is a narrow road you can use right now.
- The other is a highway that will take months to build.

The road gets you there today. But the highway, once built, gets everyone there faster for years to come. That's the power of roundabout production. It redirects effort now to multiply progress later.

Time Transforms What's Possible

The structure of production isn't just a technical process; it's a **temporal one**. Each step in production unfolds over time. And as time passes:

- New technologies emerge.
- Consumer preferences shift.
- Resource costs change.
- And producers revise their actions based on all this.

This makes **flexibility** a critical part of success. Producers must adapt based on what they learn over time, not just what they assumed at the start.

The Foundation: Saved Resources

Longer production processes require resources up front. You need time, money, labor, and materials before any finished goods can exist. Someone has to forgo immediate consumption to make this possible.

Every capital good (every tractor, crane, or 3D printer) exists because someone delayed gratification and chose to invest in future productivity instead of present enjoyment.

An Example

Think of a dam. Building it is expensive, slow, and complex. It takes years before anyone benefits. But once complete, it generates clean electricity for decades. That one investment keeps homes lit, factories running, and cities growing. Without the patience to plan, save, and build it, none of those benefits happen.

The same logic applies everywhere, from building software to launching new supply chains. The longer and more thoughtful the production process, the more abundant and generally more affordable the final goods become.

Why This Matters

If we only focus on what we want right now, we'll never build what we need for the future. Growth requires us to think past immediate consumption:

- **Complex production takes time** to organize and execute properly.
- **Quality improvements** come from trial and error processes that can't be rushed.
- **Innovation emerges** from experimentation that may not pay off immediately.

Roundabout production isn't wasteful. It's how we multiply output and create prosperity that lasts. The more sophisticated our production processes become, the more wealth we can create for everyone.

The Bottom Line

The structure of production shows us that great things take time. The economy grows not just through instant consumption, but through patient investment, flexible planning, and the slow, deliberate building of capacity. The more steps we take before reaching the finish line, the more valuable, and plentiful, the finish line can become.

Chapter Twenty-Seven

We Must Invest In The Right Tools For The Job

One Takeaway

Capital goods aren't interchangeable. Growth depends not just on how much capital we have, but whether we're using the right tools for the job.

What Are Capital Goods?

Capital goods are tools, machines, buildings, and other resources businesses use to produce goods and services for creation, not for consumption. You don't eat a hammer or drive a tractor for fun (usually). These goods are used to make other goods.

They're the tools that help us turn raw materials into value. But not all tools are created equal.

Capital Isn't One Big Blob

One of the biggest mistakes people make in thinking about capital is **assuming it's all identical**. That more of it is always better, or that any kind of capital can be thrown at any problem.

But economics teaches us the opposite. **Capital is diverse**. One tool can't always substitute for another. Hammers aren't screwdrivers. A lawn mower can't replace a computer chip. A tractor isn't going to help you build a bridge like a crane would.

Capital matters when it fits the task at hand.

Why This Matters

The specific nature of capital has serious implications:

- **Not all capital is useful everywhere.** Having lots of one kind of machine or tool doesn't help if the task requires something else entirely.
- **Bad matches can waste resources.** If capital is invested in the wrong tools, in the wrong industries, or in the wrong places, it ends up sitting idle. That's not growth. It's stagnation.
- **Misallocated capital can do more harm than good.** Overbuilding in one area while underinvesting in another doesn't lead to balance. It leads to bottlenecks, shortages, and lost opportunity.

Capital only becomes productive when it aligns with the specific demands of a project. That's why the price system and real-time feedback are so critical. They guide decisions about where and how to invest.

A Kitchen Example

Let's say you have $3,000 to equip your kitchen. If you spend it all on blenders, you're going to have a tough time making a steak dinner. **The value of your kitchen isn't just in the dollar amount of your tools.** It's in whether you have the right tools to make what you want to make.

The same is true in an economy. An economy full of misfit capital—outdated machinery, misplaced infrastructure, or tech that no one needs—isn't positioned for growth. What matters is **fitness for purpose**, not just quantity.

The Role of Markets in Matching Capital

Markets, when left to operate freely, solve this alignment problem through:

- **Prices** that help communicate which capital is valuable and which is not.

- **Profit and loss** which guides businesses toward productive uses and away from wasteful ones.

- **Entrepreneurs** who constantly experiment, adjust, and use resources based on feedback.

Without these signals, and the process of **trial and error**, we're left guessing. When we guess wrong, entire industries or economies can drift off course.

Why "Capital Stock" Can Be Misleading

You might hear phrases like "we need to invest in our capital stock" as if capital were just a big pile of stuff. But this mindset glosses over what really matters: **how well that capital fits current production needs.**

A government might build dozens of factories in remote regions and claim that it's good for economic development. But without skilled workers, transportation networks, or demand for the goods, those factories won't generate value. They'll collect dust and waste resources that could have been used elsewhere.

The Bottom Line

We need investment in the right tools in the right places, guided by the right signals. Capital is not just a number. It's a network of tools, built with purpose, and used with care. If we want long-term growth, we need more than just investment.

Chapter Twenty-Eight

We Have To Pay For Time

One Takeaway

Interest rates are the reward we get for delaying consumption now, and the price we pay to borrow from the future.

The Trade-off Between Now and Later

Every choice about saving or spending reflects a personal trade-off between the present and the future (see Ch. 25). This trade off is known as time preference. This might seem like a topic for psychology, but the idea of time preference can shape entire economies.

When lots of people have **low time preference** (they're willing to wait), there's generally more funding available for long-term projects. When most people have **high time preference** (they want things now), money tends to become scarce for investment, and economic progress can slow.

Why Savings Are the Bridge

Savings are essential because they're the bridge between consumption and production. Think of savings not as money sitting idle, but as resources being redirected from immediate use to future productivity.

Without savings, there's less available resources in the economy to be used for **investments.** This means there's less funds available to build factories, launch new ideas, or develop long-term projects. Imagine a business that spends every dollar the day it comes in. There's no room to invest in something bigger tomorrow because everything's being consumed today.

How Savings Turn Into Growth

When people save, their money doesn't just sit idle. It enters the economy through:

- Deposits in banks
- Purchases of stocks and bonds
- Contributions to retirement or investment accounts

These savings become the fuel for investment. With more deposits, banks can lend more money to businesses. Businesses then use the money to build, expand, and innovate.

But here's the key: this process takes time. **Investment is delayed consumption.** It requires confidence that the resources we set aside today will create something more valuable tomorrow.

Interest Rates: The Signal That Coordinates Time

Interest rates are how the economy balances time preferences and investment opportunities. They're both the price borrowers pay for money and the reward savers receive for waiting.

- **When savings are plentiful**, market interest rates tend to fall. Borrowing becomes easier and less costly. This encourages businesses to invest in longer-term, more complex projects.

- **When savings are scarce**, market interest rates tend to rise. Loans become expensive. Only the most promising long-term projects can justify the cost.

Think of interest rates as signals that help coordinate decisions across time. They tell entrepreneurs whether enough people are saving today to support the demand they expect tomorrow. Interest rates can also signal back to savers that entrepreneurs want to work on big plans, like housing developments or technological advances, for the future and it may be worth saving now for future gain.

Why Consumption Alone Can't Drive Growth

You'll often hear that spending more is the path to economic growth. **But while spending creates activity, it doesn't create productive capacity.** Buying new clothes doesn't increase future potential output. Building the machines that make clothes faster and better does.

- **Spending without saving** generates short-term activity.
- **Saving and investing** increases funds available to build long-term production.

Lasting growth comes from increasing our ability to produce more efficiently. That means building tools, equipment, and infrastructure. These are all essential make more goods and services in the future.

A Simple Example

Picture a carpenter who wants to grow their business:

- With only hand tools, they can build one piece of furniture a day.
- If they save enough to buy power tools, they can triple their output and maybe hire help.

That doesn't just help the carpenter. It helps their customers, their suppliers, and the broader economy. All because they used savings to invest.

The same principle scales up. Households across the country save. Banks channel those savings to businesses. Those businesses use the money to build factories, develop new technologies, and expand operations. That's how economies grow over time.

The Danger of Skipping the Wait

Some economic thinking treats savings as a problem to be solved. Some claim that consumption should be "stimulated" at all costs. But short-term consumption can't replace the long-term benefits of savings. Without saved resources, we can't build the systems and capital goods that improve living standards.

A household that spends everything it earns lives paycheck to paycheck. So does an economy.

The Bottom Line

Interest rates coordinate individual time preferences with entrepreneurial opportunities. Growth takes time, patience, and genuine savings. If we want to produce more, innovate more, and live better—not just now but in the future—we need systems that accurately reflect how much people are willing to wait. Every dollar saved and invested is a choice to build something bigger in the future, and interest rates help ensure those choices align with real opportunities.

Chapter Twenty-Nine

We Are Uncertain If We Will Profit

One Takeaway

Markets work because people try things. Sometimes they win, sometimes they lose. But, every outcome reveals what's valuable and what isn't.

Embracing the Unknown

Every decision we make about the future involves **uncertainty.** You can plan, prepare, and guess, but you'll never know exactly what will happen next. That's true in life, and it's especially true in economics. Entrepreneurs embrace the unknown by trying new ideas. Some may think what entrepreneurs do is risky. But, risk isn't quite the right word. A better word in this case is uncertainty.

Economists make an important distinction here:

Risk is when you can measure the odds. Like flipping a coin or rolling dice.

Uncertainty is when there are no set odds to measure. Like starting a new business, entering a new market, or launching a product.

In the real world, most meaningful decisions involve **uncertainty, not measurable probabilities.**

Profit and Loss: The Market's Scorecard

Every time you act in a market, whether as a business owner, a worker, or a consumer, you're placing a bet on what you think is most valuable. That bet might pay off (profit), or it might not (loss). Either way, you learn something.

- **Profit** means you created value. Your product or service met a real need.

- **Loss** means your resources could have been used better elsewhere. You took a shot and it didn't work.

It's not personal. It's a feedback loop. **Profits reward good judgment and actions. Losses expose bad ones.**

This is how the economy figures out what works and people learn how to produce things others value.

Uncertainty Makes Entrepreneurship Possible

Entrepreneurs are the people who step into the unknown. They make bets no one else is willing or able to make. They look at the world, spot a gap, and try to fill it—without any guarantee of success. Entrepreneurs:

- **Coordinate resources without being told.**

- **Take chances with their own time and money.**

- **Discover what consumers want before anyone else does.**

Without uncertainty, there would be no opportunity. If everything were known in advance, there would be no need for entrepreneurs at all.

A Simple Example

You buy a food truck and plan to sell gourmet grilled cheese sandwiches. You think people will love them. You find a great location. You test your recipes. You print menus. You start selling.

- If people line up, you earn profits and maybe expand to a second truck or a permanent location.

- If the response is lukewarm, you learn. Maybe the price is too high. Maybe the neighborhood isn't a good fit. Maybe grilled cheese isn't as exciting as you thought.

Either way, the market has given you feedback. Profit means keep going. Loss means pivot or stop.

You've gained knowledge that helps you, and others, make better decisions next time.

Why This Matters

Uncertainty, profit, and loss aren't just quirks of markets. They're essential for markets to work. Taken together they:

- **Reveal what people value.**

- **Encourage new thinking.**

- **Prevent continued waste by signaling when something isn't working.**

When we remove profit and loss from a system we lose that feedback. And when people don't face uncertainty, they stop learning.

The Market as a Discovery Process

Think of the economy as a giant experiment. Millions of people try things every day. Some succeed. Some fail. But every outcome teaches us something.

- **Profits don't just enrich entrepreneurs; they show what should be done based on what's available and what consumers value.**
- **Losses don't just hurt; they show what shouldn't be done.**

Over time, this process moves resources toward more valuable uses. That's how progress happens.

The Bottom Line

Markets turn real-world uncertainty into information. Every decision, win or lose, helps us understand what people want and how to serve them better. The best thing we can do is pay attention to the signals and keep trying.

Chapter Thirty

We Learn What Works By Trying

One Takeaway

Entrepreneurs move the economy forward. They don't follow a map. But they do spot new paths no one else may see and take a chance to walk them.

The Entrepreneur's Role

Economies don't grow on autopilot. Someone has to take the leap. Someone must start the business, test the product, build the thing that doesn't yet exist. That someone is the **entrepreneur.**

Entrepreneurs are not just business owners. They're decision-makers. Chance-takers. Problem-solvers. They coordinate people, resources, and ideas to create something new in a world that offers no guarantees.

More than anything, they act. And in doing so, they shape the future.

Entrepreneurs Are Alert

Some people walk past an empty lot and see weeds. Others see a future coffee shop.

That's **alertness**—the ability to notice what's missing, what could be better, or what's about to change. Entrepreneurs are constantly scanning the world for **unmet needs** or **underused opportunities.**

- A growing neighborhood with no childcare provider.
- A product that's good, but could be great with one tweak.
- A process that's clunky, and ripe for a better way.

This kind of awareness isn't luck. It's practiced, intentional, and essential. **Entrepreneurs add value by offering something better, faster, cheaper, or completely new.**

Entrepreneurs Use Judgment

Once an opportunity is spotted, there's a second hurdle: action.

Entrepreneurs act based on **judgment**, not certainty. They use **incomplete information** to make bets about the future. And they do it in real time before they know what the "right" answer is.

Judgment is what separates talkers from doers. Anyone can say, "That should exist." The entrepreneur is the one who builds it. If it works, they profit. If it doesn't, they lose.

Either way, the outcome helps everyone learn what brings value to customers, and, importantly, what doesn't.

Entrepreneurs Throw Out the Old

Progress doesn't come without tradeoffs. New ideas can sweep in and replace old ones. That's what some economists call **creative destruction**.

Streaming services replace cable. Smartphones replace landlines. Ride-share apps replace taxis. These shifts are disruptive, but they also make life better.

- Consumers win with better, cheaper, more convenient options.
- Resources move from outdated industries to new opportunities.
- Entrepreneurs benefit by leading the change.

Creative destruction can be painful. Jobs change. Companies close. But long-term prosperity depends on this cycle of renewal.

Entrepreneurship is a Function, Not a Title

You don't need a business card that says "founder" to be entrepreneurial. What matters is the types of actions you make in the economy.

Entrepreneurs:

- Use the price system to guide their decisions.
- Turn abstract knowledge into real-world solutions.
- Create value by thinking differently and acting boldly.

They don't wait for permission. They act when others hesitate.

Why This Matters

Entrepreneurs keep the economy from standing still. Without them, we wouldn't have innovation, job creation, or economic growth.

But none of this is guaranteed. Entrepreneurship requires a system that rewards experimentation and allows failure. That means we need:

- Market prices that reflect reality
- Freedom to try (and fail)
- Absence of barriers that discourage starting a business or that slow down innovation

The Bottom Line

Entrepreneurs shape the market and are the sources of growth for the economy. They discover what's possible and create new ways to serve others. Their alertness, judgment, and willingness to destroy the old to make way for the new are what keep our economy dynamic, resilient, and alive.

Chapter Thirty-One

Short Answer: We Can't Shortcut Time And Learning

What It Actually Took to Open That Coffee Shop

You walk into your favorite coffee shop and it feels simple. A counter, a menu, a person who hands you a cup. But behind that simplicity is a story about time, risk, and patience that most customers never see.

The owner — let's call her Elena — didn't wake up one day and open a shop. She saved for three years while working as a barista at someone else's café. She was producing and earning before she was spending and building. Every dollar she set aside was a dollar she didn't spend on something she wanted today, because she wanted something bigger tomorrow.

When she finally had enough, she faced a choice that looked simple but wasn't. A commercial espresso machine cost $12,000. A consumer model cost $3,000. The cheap one would probably work. But it would slow down service during the morning rush. It might produce inconsistent coffee. It would definitely need to be replaced within two years. She invested in the right tool for the job, knowing the return wouldn't show up for months.

Then she waited. The first six months, she lost money. Her business plan said she'd break even in four months, but the plan was wrong. Foot traffic was slower than expected. Her original menu had fourteen drinks.

She learned over time that people mostly wanted five. She cut the rest. She moved the pastry case closer to the register and sales jumped. None of this was in the plan. She figured it out by trying, failing, and adjusting.

She couldn't have skipped any of this. She couldn't have borrowed her way past the learning curve, or franchised someone else's concept and gotten the same result, or received a government grant that replaced the knowledge she gained from six months of mistakes. The saving, the investing, the waiting, the uncertainty, the trial and error. Each step was hard. But each step was essential. Remove any one of them and the shop you walk into every morning doesn't exist.

Now apply this to the next shortcut you're offered. Someone promises fast returns with minimal risk. Someone else says a program will create prosperity by injecting money into the right places. Ask what Elena would ask: where's the production? How's it being funded? Who's bearing the uncertainty? How long has this had to prove itself?

The places and businesses that create real, lasting value all share the same foundation. Someone produced before they consumed. Someone saved before they spent. Someone accepted uncertainty, acted, then waited. There are rarely ever exceptions to these steps. Anyone selling you one is almost certainly offering a shortcut that isn't one.

Why Can't We Make The Economy Do What We Want?

Why can't smart leaders just take the reins and make the economy grow? The temptation is understandable: if we know the ingredients that create wealth, surely we can manage the recipe. But it's not that simple. To understand why, we need to confront some uncomfortable truths about knowledge, complexity, and the limits of control.

EconomicsFor

Chapter Thirty-Two

We Can't Outsmart The System

One Takeaway

The economy runs on signals, not switches. The more we try to control outcomes from the top down, the more we distort the very signals that help people make good decisions from the ground up.

Messing With Signals Messes With the System

If you could push a button to raise your income, lower unemployment, or make your money worth more, wouldn't that be nice?

That's the promise a lot of economic policy tries to sell: twist a few knobs, set some rates, pass the right bill and *poof* the economy will do what we want. But the truth is, the economy isn't a machine with levers and dials. It's a system of people. And every person is acting, choosing, reacting, and adapting based on the signals around them.

Change those signals, and you change the choices.

This means the tools some choose to use to "manage the economy" (interest rates, inflation targets, stimulus packages) aren't neutral. They shape behavior. And the consequences can mislead the very people the economy depends on.

Coordination Without a Conductor

Markets work not because anyone is in charge, but because everyone is adjusting to everyone else.

That's the real beauty of systems without central control. You don't need a master plan. **You need clear signals.** Prices tell us where things are scarce. Interest rates tell us whether people are saving or spending. Profits and losses tell us whether we're creating value or wasting resources.

These are vital pieces of information.

They help us answer essential questions: Should I invest now or wait? Should I hire more people or cut back? Should I move to this city, change careers, buy a home?

What Happens When The Signals Are Wrong?

In 2005, families across the U.S. looked at the numbers and made what seemed like a smart decision. Interest rates were low. Housing values seemed to never stop climbing. Their monthly payment on a new home would barely be more than rent. Every signal said: buy now.

So, they did. And so did millions of others.

But those signals were misleading. Interest rates weren't low because Americans were saving more. They were low because the Federal Reserve had pushed them there. Housing prices weren't climbing because of real demand. They were climbing because cheap credit flooded the market with buyers who couldn't actually afford what they were purchasing.

When rates adjusted and the credit dried up, homes lost significant amounts of their value. Monthly payments jumped. Owners got stuck owing more than the house was worth.

These families didn't make bad decisions. **They made reasonable de-**

cisions based on bad information. That's exactly what distorted signals do. They turn good judgment into bad outcomes across millions of people at once.

Why Some Try Anyway

So why do we keep trying to manage the system from the top?

Because it's tempting. Big problems seem to call for big solutions. And aggregates like GDP, inflation, and unemployment give the illusion of control and a complete picture. They turn a messy, dynamic system into a scoreboard. And if you think you can move the score by adjusting a few settings, why not try?

But the scoreboard isn't the game. When you focus too much on moving the numbers, you forget about the players. You forget about the incentives, the trade-offs, the limits, the local knowledge. You forget the stuff that actually makes the economy work.

Good Rules Beat Good Intentions

This doesn't mean we throw up our hands and do nothing. But it means we focus on what can work.

We don't need a better pilot. We need a better autopilot. That means:

- Clear, stable rules people can rely on.
- Sound money that holds its value over time.
- Prices that reflect reality, not someone's best guess.
- Freedom to adjust, innovate, fail, and try again.

When we focus on those things, the system works surprisingly well and better than any other alternative. Not because we control it. But instead, because we've stopped trying to.

The Bottom Line

Every attempt to manage the economy from the top-down risks distorting the signals people rely on to make good decisions. It's true that you can't manage something if you can't measure it. But it's also true that just because you can measure something does not automatically mean it needs to be managed.

Chapter Thirty-Three

We Need More Than Headlines

One Takeaway

Statistics like GDP are helpful summaries, but they offer limited explanations of how the economy is doing. Without a crystal ball to predict the future, it's better to focus on principles than managing statistics.

The Number Everyone Talks About

Maybe last night's news told you that GDP is expected to grow by this next quarter. Good news...right?

Maybe. GDP adds up everything we spend. This includes whether we're building a new business or replacing a flooded basement. Both count the same in GDP stats. **More spending sometimes is progress and other times only looks like progress.** Not all spending makes us better off.

That doesn't mean GDP isn't helpful. It means it's a summary, not a story. And summaries need someone who knows how to read them. The same is true for every economic stat you hear on the news. Once you know what questions to ask, you'll be able to understand them better than most.

What the Numbers Can Miss

Take unemployment. The headline might say 4%. That sounds healthy. But behind that number are six different ways the government measures unemployment. The most narrow measures only long-term job seekers. The most broad includes part-time workers who want full-time jobs and people who've stopped looking entirely. Depending on which measure you use, the story can change.

A falling unemployment rate could mean new jobs are being created. Or it could mean people gave up looking. The unemployment number alone doesn't tell you which.

Or inflation. The news says 3%. But your rent went up 10% and your grocery bill climbed 5%. Meanwhile, the price of your TV dropped. The official number averages all of that together. Your lived experience of inflation and the reported number can feel like they're describing two different economies.

These numbers aren't wrong. Taken alone in a headline they're just incomplete. And that's an important difference. **The problem isn't the stats themselves. It's treating them like the full picture when they're really a sketch.**

The Right Questions Change Explanations

You don't need a degree in economics or data analysis to understand these data points. You simply need to start with questions that most people don't think of when they hear a headline number.

When you hear GDP grew: Ask whether that growth came from productive investment or from spending that replaced something lost.

When you hear unemployment fell: Ask what's happening underneath. Are people finding work they want? Or are they settling, or giving up?

When you hear inflation is "under control": Ask in what way? If you're a retiree on a fixed income and food and medical costs are climbing, a low headline number doesn't describe your reality.

The numbers are summaries. The human decisions and actions behind them are the full picture.

Why This Matters Beyond Your Living Room

These aren't just questions for you to ask while watching the news. They're the same questions policymakers should be asking. The trouble is they most often aren't.

When a government designs a program to "reduce unemployment," it's targeting a number. But if that number can fall for reasons that have nothing to do with people finding good work, then hitting the target doesn't mean they solved the problem. When a central bank promises to "control inflation," it's managing an average. But if that average hides the fact that housing and food costs are surging while electronics get cheaper, the policy might look successful on paper while families feel squeezed.

This is one reason we can't simply make the economy do what we want. The tools we use to measure success are helpful, but are blunter than many believe them to be. When we build policies around moving a number, we risk improving the scoreboard without improving the game.

GDP growth is great, but not if it comes at a loss to lives, liberty, and livelihood.

Why Predictions Fail But Principles Don't

It's tempting to think that better numbers would lead to better predictions. If we just measured more precisely, we could see what's coming more clearly. But the economy is made up of millions of people making plans, changing their minds, and responding to each other in real time. That's not a system that lends itself to perfect forecasting.

Economic statistics can help us spot broad trends over time, compare approaches in similar situations, and identify problems that need attention. These are genuinely useful. But they can't tell us what caused what without deeper analysis. They also can't predict what comes next.

That's why principles and foundations matter more than predictions. Understanding how prices work, why people cooperate, and what drives growth helps you adapt to whatever comes next. A headline number can't do that. How you think about that number can.

The Bottom Line

Economic statistics are guides, not answers. They can sketch the outline of what's happening, but they can't paint the full picture. The best economic thinking doesn't try to predict what the numbers will say next. It gives you the principles to understand what the numbers mean and what they miss.

Chapter Thirty-Four

We Each Know Different Things (And No One Knows Everything)

One Takeaway

No one person has all the knowledge in the world. The best systems are those that help us use what we know to make better decisions.

Who Knows What We Should Do?

Every day, people make decisions based on things only they know. How long the commute is that day, whether their kid is getting sick, how much their neighbor might pay for a used bike. These tiny pieces of knowledge may not seem like much, but they're everywhere. And they matter.

The central challenge in economics is figuring out how to make the best use of all this spread-out knowledge. The real question isn't, "What should we do?" It's, "Who knows enough to decide what should be done?"

What Is The Knowledge Problem?

No single person or authority can know enough to make good decisions for everyone else. This is a very simplified version of what's known as the **knowledge problem**.

Knowledge is spread out. It lives in the minds of millions of individuals, each with access to their own slice of information. This knowledge is often based on **time**, **place**, **habits**, and **situations** no outsider could ever fully grasp. Because of this, we all know some things, but no one knows all of it.

Different Kinds of Knowledge

To see why this matters, it helps to distinguish between different types of knowledge:

- **General Knowledge:** Broad principles like how engines work or that too much pesticide can kill plants.

- **Local Knowledge:** Information specific to a particular time and place. Something like knowing that customers in your neighborhood prefer different groceries when it's hot out.

- **Tacit Knowledge:** Skills and insights you have but can't easily explain. Like knowing when bread dough feels "right," or sensing when a customer is about to buy.

All three types matter. But local and tacit knowledge are the hardest for others to access and make use of.

The Wal-Mart Example

During Hurricane Katrina, Wal-Mart's disaster response for getting supplies to the region outperformed government agencies. While FEMA waited for damage reports and approval processes, local Wal-Mart managers sprung into action. Among other actions, these managers verified which roads were passable by going and inspecting them. This allowed them to route deliveries correctly. This information didn't exist in any government database. It took on the ground, second-to-second data.

Wal-Mart had supplies arriving before FEMA had even finished its assessment. They achieved this because they had **systems that trusted and enabled people with local knowledge to make local decisions.**

Why Local Knowledge Beats Central Plans

This is why local decision-makers can repeatedly outperform distant authorities. They see changes as they happen. They understand local trade-offs. And they know details that never make it into official reports.

For example:

- A store manager likely understands the buying habits of local customers better than the company's CEO. If a retail chain mandates the same winter inventory across the U.S., stores in hot and cold climates might end up with the same amount and types of coats. The result? Unsold goods in one state and empty shelves in another.

- A farmer knows the specific conditions of their land (soil quality, weather, and pest risks) better than a policymaker miles away.

- A teacher knows which students learn better through visuals versus through discussion. This knowledge doesn't show up in standardized test data.

Making decisions from too far away means making decisions without being able to see what truly matters.

When General Knowledge Isn't Enough

While general knowledge is important, it has limits. General principles are certainly helpful, but they must be applied with care at the local level.

For example, McDonald's has general guidelines for their service. But how they put those guidelines in place differs across the globe. In some markets they may not serve beef, or they may offer table service. No matter what, the general principle of fast, consistent food service stays the same. But knowing the right way to apply the knowledge changes.

How Markets Solve the Knowledge Problem

Markets don't solve this problem by giving one person more knowledge. They solve it by not needing to.

Prices, profits, and losses carry information. **They do all this without anyone having to centrally process, verify, and approve every data point and fact or opinion.**

When a restaurant owner sees that fish prices have jumped, she doesn't need to understand if global fishing regulations are to blame. She just knows fish is expensive today. Maybe that means tonight's special should be chicken instead.

The beauty of markets is that they bring together all this spread-out knowledge without requiring anyone to collect it.

The Bottom Line

No one knows everything, but everyone knows something. Good systems don't concentrate decision-making at the top. They build feedback loops that let each person act on what they know best. When people are free to use their knowledge, outcomes across the economy improve.

Chapter Thirty-Five

We Don't Control What Others Own

One Takeaway

Property rights make exchange, investment, and cooperation possible. Without them, markets can’t function and progress stalls.

The Garden You Won't Plant

Imagine you rent a small house with a bare backyard. You'd love to plant a garden, but your lease is month-to-month, and your landlord has been talking about selling the property.

So, you don't plant anything. Why invest weeks of work and money if someone else might benefit from it, or worse, tear it all out next month?

That hesitation isn't laziness. It's rational. You're responding to the fact that you don't have a secure claim on the outcome of your effort. Without confidence that what you build will remain yours, you won't build.

Now scale that feeling up to an entire economy, and you start to see why property rights matter so much.

What Property Rights Are

Property rights are the rules that define who can use something, benefit from it, and transfer it to someone else. They apply to physical things like land, tools, inventory, and to intangible things like ideas, contracts, and creative work.

But property rights aren't just about legal ownership. They're a bundle of expectations:

- Can I use this resource the way I see fit?
- Will I benefit from improving it?
- Can I sell it, trade it, or give it away?
- Will someone protect my claim if it's challenged?

When these expectations are clear and reliable, people invest, plan, and cooperate. When they aren't, people protect what they have rather than building something new.

Why Economics Depends on This

Throughout this book, we've talked about prices, trade, saving, investment, and entrepreneurship. Every one of these depends on property rights functioning in the background.

You can only sell something if it's yours to sell. A buyer can only pay for something if the money they're offering belongs to them.

Trade requires transferability. If you can't transfer what's yours to someone who values it more, trade doesn't happen. Without trade, we lose the gains from specialization, comparative advantage, and cooperation that make prosperity possible.

Investment requires security. No one puts money into a business, a piece of land, or someone's education if the returns can be taken or the rules can change without warning. The carpenter who saves to buy power tools in order to produce more only does so because he expects to keep the benefit of that investment.

Entrepreneurship requires the right to try. Starting a business means rearranging resources in a new way. That requires the freedom to obtain and use property based on your own judgment about what might work.

Remove any of these and the entire system we've been describing slows down or stops.

The Tragedy of No Ownership

When nobody owns a resource, nobody tends to take care of it.

Consider a public park with no maintenance budget and no one assigned to look after it. Trash builds up. Equipment breaks. People stop visiting. This happened because no one had the incentive or the authority to maintain it.

The same logic applies to fisheries where no one owns the fish. Forests where no one owns the trees. And aquifers where no one owns the water. When everyone can take but no one is responsible, resources get used up faster than they can recover.

This isn't because people are greedy. It's because the incentives point in the wrong direction. **Ownership aligns the person using the resource with the long-term consequences of how they use it.** Without that alignment, short-term thinking wins every time.

Property rights can start informally. Families establish norms about shared spaces. Communities develop customs about water use or grazing land. Online platforms create reputation systems that function like property protections for digital sellers.

Formal legal systems can, and should, strengthen and extend these arrangements. But the instinct to define "what's mine" and "what's yours" tends to show up wherever and whenever people cooperate. It's not a product of government invention. It's a foundation of human coordination that governments can either support or undermine.

The Bottom Line

Property rights make the rest of economics work. They give people the confidence to invest, the ability to trade, the incentive to maintain what they have, and the freedom to try something new. When property is secure, people think long-term. When it isn't, they think about survival.

Chapter Thirty-Six

We Can't Calculate Without Prices

One Takeaway

Without prices that reflect reality, no one, not even the smartest, most informed planner, can know how best to use scarce resources.

How Do We Decide What to Make and How Much of It?

Imagine trying to bake and sell bread without knowing what flour costs. Or deciding to build a bridge without knowing whether steel or concrete is cheaper. These situations sound far-fetched, but they are more common in history than people realize, and they lie at the core of what some economists call the **calculation problem**.

Economic calculation is how producers make decisions. It's how they answer basic but essential questions:

- What should we produce?
- How should we produce it?
- How much should we produce?

To answer these questions, producers rely on prices. Prices reflect information about scarcity, alternatives, and consumer wants. Prices condense millions of choices into a simple signal that anyone can use.

The Information Hidden in Every Price

Every price tells a story you could never learn any other way. For example, the price of copper reflects:

- How much copper exists in known mines
- How difficult it is to extract and refine
- What industries need copper right now
- What substitutes are available
- What people expect copper prices to be tomorrow

No single person knows all this. But the price captures it all. When copper gets more expensive, construction companies may start using more plastic pipes. Electronics manufacturers may look for alternatives.

Markets Handle This Best

In markets, prices emerge from exchange. Buyers and sellers interact, each using their own knowledge, wants, and limits. The result? Prices that reflect reality, even if no one understands all the pieces.

In economies where governments own inputs like raw materials, machinery, or labor, there are no real prices. **Without ownership and competition, there's no true exchange.** Planners are left with no alternative other than to guess at values, set quotas, and hope for the best. This is where things go wrong.

Without market prices, which rely on property rights and voluntary exchange, resources don't flow where they're most needed. Producers then can't tell whether they're creating value or wasting effort. Eventually, growth halts, because no one gets a clear signal about what's working.

A Tale of Two Bakeries

Let's say you own a bakery. In a market, you buy flour based on demand. If demand surges, you bake more. If it drops, you bake less. While producing, you track the price inputs like flour, butter, electricity, and wages. If flour prices spike, you might switch to recipes that use less flour, or you might try to charge more, if customers are willing and able to pay.

Now imagine you run a bakery under a system without prices. The government gives the same amount of flour to everyone, both bakers and non-bakers. You don't know what flour costs, or how scarce it is, or if someone else needs it more. If you produce too much, it goes to waste. If too little, customers' needs aren't met. When flour becomes scarce, you have no way to know until you run out, or it stops coming.

That's the calculation problem. **It's not a math error; it's a knowledge error.** Without prices, there's no way to know what choices make sense.

The Soviet Steel Mill Problem

Here's a real-world example of what happens without prices. In the Soviet Union, the government set production targets for steel mills to meet. They said something like "produce 1,000 tons of steel goods." Sounds reasonable, maybe? But without market prices to guide them, the mills had no way to know what *kind* of steel goods consumers needed.

So, they made what seemed easiest. They made thousands of thick, heavy sheets and enormous nails. These met their weight quotas, but the products weren't useful for much (what are you going to do with a 20 lb. nail?). Meanwhile, other producers needed thin steel for machinery and small nails for roofing. The mills produced millions of tons of steel goods nobody needed. **The producers were paid for making things no one needed.**

Why? Because tons of steel aren't the same as the right tons of steel. Without prices to signal what consumers valued, there was no way for the mills to know the difference, or really to care.

When Prices Lie, Decisions Fail

Even in markets, problems arise when prices don't reflect reality. Suppose the government pays some of the cost of corn production. This allows producers to get away with cheaper prices. Suddenly:

- Food companies use more corn syrup instead of sugar
- Farmers plant corn instead of vegetables
- Ethanol producers use corn for fuel instead of food

These decisions make sense based on the low price. But they're actually wasteful. We end up using corn for things that aren't worth its real cost.

The Bottom Line

Prices must come from exchanges not by decree. The more people that own and exchange goods the more information is reflected in prices. Without ownership and exchange, prices don't exist. If prices don't exist, no one can figure out if what they are producing is helpful or wasteful. Without prices, planning is guessing. With prices, it's calculation. And calculation is what keeps the economy moving forward.

Chapter Thirty-Seven

We Need Good Rules More Than Good Rulers

One Takeaway

A successful and growing economy depends more on good rules than wise overseers. Clear, consistent institutions allow people to cooperate, plan, and adapt without having anyone in charge.

The Game Works Well When the Rules Are Clear

Most of the time, when we think of what makes an economy work, we picture active players: entrepreneurs, workers, investors, consumers. But behind every decision they make is something easy to miss: **the rules of the game.**

Rules shape actions. In soccer, you can't use your hands. In chess, each piece moves a certain way. The same is true in the economy. The rules, whether written or unwritten, determine what kinds of decisions are possible, encouraged, or punished. Economists call these rules "**institutions**."

Institutions are the invisible skeleton that holds the economy together. Think of things like:

- Property rights
- Contract enforcement
- Banking laws and trust in the currency
- Cultural norms of fairness or reputation

When institutions work well, the economy just *feels* like it works. People trade, invest, and build for the future. **When institutions break down, even smart people with the best intentions struggle to get anything done.**

Why Institutions Matter

Imagine two cities. In one, there are clear rules, honest courts, and stable money. In the other, property can be seized without warning, contracts are never written down, and money loses value overnight.

In which society would you rather:

- Start a business?
- Save for retirement?
- Lend money to a friend?

In the first society, you can plan. In the second, you just try to survive.

That's the power of institutions. They reduce uncertainty. They help strangers cooperate rather than conflict with each other. They allow value to be stored over time. And they give people the confidence to try new things. That's what makes them foundational to long-run prosperity.

Good Rules Matter Most

People often think the solution to economic problems is to elect the "right leader." Someone who will fix everything with wisdom and fairness.

But no matter how smart a ruler is, they face the same problem we all do: limited knowledge and self-interest. No matter how great they are, they aren't an all-knowing angel. Even well-meaning leaders can't replace the information embedded in millions of scattered decisions.

That's why good rules are better than good rulers.

Rules don't have to be perfect, but they certainly can be better or worse. Ideally the rules need to be clear, consistent, and applied the same way no matter who, when, or where an issue may come up. When they are applied consistently and in a predictable way, people can take chances, make deals, and adjust as circumstances change.

Institutions in Everyday Life

You experience institutions every day without even noticing.

When you swipe your card at a store and it goes through? That's a system of **financial and legal trust**.

When you sign a lease or work contract and expect it to be honored? That's **contract enforcement**.

When you buy from a stranger on the internet and expect the product to arrive? That's a mix of **reputation systems**, **third-party guarantees**, and **social norms**.

None of this works because someone plans every action. It works because people built, maintained, and followed institutions. These institutions almost always evolve over time, rather than being invented overnight.

The Cost of Weak Institutions

What happens when institutions are weak, inconsistent, or corrupt?

- **Bribes may replace rules.** Decisions go to the connected, not the capable.

- **Investment can dry up.** No one builds for the long term if tomorrow is uncertain.
- **Talent often runs away.** Entrepreneurs and skilled workers go where their efforts are protected.
- **Wealth quickly stagnates.** Not because people don't want to try, but because the system doesn't reward good decisions.
- **Weak institutions are a tax on human progress.** They punish those who want to play by the rules by changing the rules halfway through.

Institutions Are Built, Not Given

Strong institutions don't appear by magic. They're shaped by history, politics, culture, technology, and incentives. Some evolve informally—like trust. Others sometimes require formal systems—like courts.

The key insight? **We must be humble about how much we can engineer institutions from scratch.** Like language or markets, they often emerge through trial, error, and iteration.

But once in place, they're incredibly powerful. They allow free people to cooperate without being controlled by having a predictable means of addressing conflict.

The Bottom Line

A healthy economy depends less on heroic leaders than on good rules that work quietly in the background. Institutions make trade, trust, and time possible. They shape the incentives and expectations that guide human action. Markets don't need to be managed, but they do need to be made possible. And that starts with the right institutions.

Chapter Thirty-Eight

Short Answer: We Know More Than Any Planner Can

What If Someone Else Decided Where You Get Your Coffee?

Imagine your city council decides there are too many coffee shops in some neighborhoods and not enough in others. They commission a study, hire consultants, and create a Coffee Distribution Plan. New permits will be issued based on population density, traffic patterns, and average income data. The goal is efficiency and equity: the right number of shops in the right places. It sounds...reasonable. But now you have five questions to ask before you trust the plan.

1. **What local knowledge does this override?** Elena, from our last Short Answer, opened her shop on a quiet side street because she noticed that parents walking kids to school needed a stop along the route. That insight doesn't appear in any population density study. The consultant's data says her block is underserved by foot traffic metrics. Elena's eyes say otherwise. **Before you trust the plan, ask: what do the people on the ground know that the planners can't see from a spreadsheet?**

2. **Where are the real prices, and are they being replaced with guesses?** Elena pays rent that reflects real demand for her location. If the city starts subsidizing coffee shops in "underserved" areas, those shops don't face the same cost pressure. They don't need to earn their location. And the shops that did earn theirs now compete against subsidized alternatives. **Ask: is this plan using real signals or overriding them?**

3. **How will people adapt, and has anyone thought about that?** If permits are capped in popular neighborhoods, entrepreneurs won't just accept the limit. Some will open "bakeries" that happen to serve coffee. Others will set up carts just outside the restricted zone. Customers will drive further, creating the traffic congestion the plan was supposed to reduce. **Ask: what will people do if this goes into effect, not what the plan assumes they'll do?**

4. **What happens if it doesn't work?** If the subsidized shop in the underserved neighborhood fails because people there prefer tea, will the program be shut down? Or will it be expanded with a bigger budget and a new study? **Ask: is there a mechanism to stop this if it fails, or will failure just lead to more planning?**

5. **What would happen if nobody did anything?** Before the plan, Elena and other owners were already solving this problem. They opened shops where they saw opportunity. Some succeeded. Some failed. The failures freed up resources for the next person to try. **The system may have been "messy," but it was adapting and using information no study could capture.**

You won't always have all these answers. But asking them puts you ahead of almost everyone else who stops at "does this sound like a good idea?" **You now know that sounding good and working well are very different things.**

How Can Politics Shape (Or Mis-shape) The Economy?

We must think carefully about what role the government has in the economy. Political decisions affect everything from the money we use to the rules the shape our actions. When does political action help economic progress, and when does it hurt? The answer depends on understanding how political incentives differ from market incentives.

EconomicsFor

Chapter Thirty-Nine

We Thrive When Exchange Is Voluntary

One Takeaway

Voluntary exchange creates value because both sides choose to participate. When decisions are made on our behalf, even with good intentions, we lose the information and feedback that help resources go where they're needed most.

The Search for a Better Park

Let's say a few years ago, a neighborhood needed a new park. Everyone agreed the old one was in bad shape. But how to fix it became a different question entirely.

The city council proposed a $4 million renovation funded by a tax increase. The plan included a splash pad. A performance stage. A new redesigned walking trail. The mock-ups looked great.

But some residents wanted something simpler. They just wanted the old playground fixed and to have some better lighting. Others would have preferred the $4 million to go toward road repairs. A few small business owners pointed out that the tax increase would eat into the cash flow they'd been putting toward hiring.

The park got built. It looked beautiful. The splash pad was popular in the summer. But the performance stage sat mostly empty. Meanwhile, the roads didn't get fixed. Some of the business owners delayed their hires. And more than a few residents felt they'd paid for someone else's priorities.

Was the park a waste? Not exactly. Some people genuinely valued it. But the process revealed something important: **when one group makes spending decisions for everyone, some people end up paying for things they wouldn't have chosen, and the things they would have chosen don't get done.** That trade-off is real. And it's worth understanding clearly.

Why Voluntary Exchange Works So Well

Throughout this book, we've built up a picture of how markets coordinate millions of people without anyone being in charge. The key ingredient is voluntary choice.

Every time you buy something, you're saying: "I'd rather have this than keep my money." Every time a business sells something, it's saying: "I'd rather have the revenue than the product." Both sides expect to benefit. If they didn't, the exchange wouldn't happen.

This process generates enormous amounts of information. Prices tell producers what people want. Profits tell them they're getting it right. Losses tell them to adjust. The whole system runs on feedback that no one has to design or manage.

What Changes When Choices Are Made For Us

Governments currently manage many institutions in the economy. Courts enforce contracts. Laws protect property. Public infrastructure connects communities. Whether these are the only ways to provide these institutions is a deeper question, but for now, they're the foundation that makes voluntary exchange possible.

But government also makes spending decisions that go beyond this foundation. And when it does, the economics change.

Tax-funded programs replace individual choice with collective decision-making. That's not automatically bad, but it does mean we lose the feedback loop. There are no prices telling officials whether the park was worth more than the road repair. There's no profit-and-loss signal telling them the performance stage was a poor use of funds. The information that would normally guide resources toward their best use simply isn't there.

This matters because:

- Without market signals, officials have to guess what people value, and different people value very different things.

- Without profit and loss, programs that aren't working don't automatically get corrected. A private business that builds something nobody wants goes under. A government program that is unsuccessful can get a bigger budget next year.

- Without individual choice, the people paying for a decision and the people making it aren't always the same people. This changes the incentives.

The Unseen Side of Every Public Decision

This doesn't mean government programs never help anyone. They often do. But every dollar spent publicly is a dollar that was taken from someone who would have spent it differently. The community center gets built, but the business doesn't hire. The subsidy supports one industry, but consumers pay higher prices. The tariff protects one set of jobs but raises costs across the economy.

These aren't arguments against government. They're arguments for taking trade-offs as seriously as we've taken them throughout this entire book.

The relevant question at hand is whether a specific action creates more value than what it displaces. And without the feedback that voluntary exchange provides, that question is genuinely hard, if not impossible, to answer.

The Bottom Line

Voluntary exchange works because both sides choose to participate, and the signals it generates help resources flow toward their best use. When decisions are made collectively, we lose that feedback. This means even well-intentioned programs can direct resources away from where people would have sent them. Understanding the difference between chosen exchange and directed spending helps us tell whether any given intervention is helping or quietly making things harder.

Chapter Forty

We Sometimes Create Spillovers

One Takeaway

Not every cost or benefit stays between the buyer and seller. When our actions spill over onto others, understanding why it happens matters more than assuming someone needs to step in.

The Neighbor's Bonfire

Your neighbor loves weekend bonfires. He invites friends over, lights up the fire pit, and has a great time. He bought the wood. He's on his own property. The transaction between him and the firewood seller was completely voluntary. Everyone involved agreed to the deal.

But the smoke drifts into your yard. Your kids can't play outside. Your laundry on the line smells like a campfire. You didn't agree to any of this.

That smoke is an **externality.** Externalities are costs (or benefits) that land on someone who wasn't part of the original exchange. Your neighbor isn't doing anything wrong in his own mind. He made a voluntary purchase and is using his property. But the full cost of his bonfire isn't falling on him.

Part of it is falling on you.

This is one of the most common reasons people say markets are flawed. And it's worth understanding carefully, because how you think about this problem shapes how you think about solving it.

What Externalities Actually Are

Externalities come in two forms.

Negative externalities are costs that fall on someone outside the transaction. A factory that pollutes a river imposes costs on the people downstream. A loud bar imposes costs on the residents next door. The producer benefits, the customer benefits, but a third party pays a price they never agreed to.

Positive externalities are benefits that spill over to people who didn't pay for them. A neighbor who maintains a beautiful garden might raise your property value. A beekeeper's bees pollinate nearby farms. The teenager who decides to wear deodorant for the first time. The buyer and seller both benefit...and so do others who had nothing to do with the exchange.

In both cases, the price of the purchase or exchange doesn't capture the full benefits and costs across all direct and indirect parties.

The Usual Response, and Its Trade-Offs

When people encounter externalities, the instinct is to call for a rule. Tax the polluter to make up for the damage. Subsidize the beekeeper so they can do more good. Pass a law about bonfires. Detention to every smelly teen!

Sometimes that works. But it always comes with its own costs. Regulations can be captured by the people they're supposed to restrain. Taxes require someone to measure the damage accurately, which is harder than it sounds. Subsidies can encourage more of some thing than the amount people actually want. And every intervention introduces new incentives that produce their own unintended consequences.

The question isn't whether externalities are real. They are. The question is whether the solution creates fewer problems than the problem itself.

What Ownership Makes Possible

There's another way to think about this. Many externalities exist not because markets failed, but because property rights are unclear or incomplete.

If the polluted river is owned by someone, the factory can't pollute it without consequence. In that case the owner will demand compensation to offset cleaning costs or take the factory to court. If your neighbor's smoke crosses onto your property, that's a dispute that clear property rules can help resolve. When ownership is defined and enforceable, people can negotiate directly. The person causing the cost and the person bearing it can find a solution that works for both of them. Oftentimes they can do this without anyone else getting involved.

This isn't always straightforward in every case. Some problems are widely spread out. You can't easily negotiate with a million car drivers about air quality. But the principle still matters: the clearer the ownership, the fewer the spillovers go unaccounted. Many of the externalities we blame on "market failure" start with failures to define who owns what.

When Markets Solve It Themselves

Markets also develop their own solutions to spillover problems when they're allowed to. **Insurance companies** price risk in ways that incentivize safer behavior. **Reputation systems** punish businesses that impose costs on communities. **Neighborhood associations** create shared rules for shared spaces. **Industry groups** develop standards that go beyond what any regulation requires, because their credibility depends on it.

These aren't perfect. But they have something government solutions often lack: built-in feedback. When they stop working, people stop paying for them. That self-correction is valuable.

The Bottom Line

Not every cost stays between buyer and seller. That's real, and it matters. But recognizing the problem and knowing how to solve it are two different things. The best responses tend to start with clear property rights, rely on the people closest to the problem, and stay humble about unintended consequences. Externalities are a reason to think carefully, not a reason to assume that every spillover requires a new rule.

Chapter Forty-One

We Can Get Fooled By Good Intentions

One Takeaway

Public officials respond to incentives just like the rest of us. We must always remember that self-interest doesn't disappear simply because someone wants to be a public servant.

Why Good Intentions Aren't Enough

Many times, we expect governments to act like wise caretakers. We want them to be objective, farsighted, and selfless. We often assume or hope that once someone is elected to office or appointed to a public agency, they stop being self-interested and start working solely for the public good.

But that's not how people work. And it just so happens that politicians, regulators, and bureaucrats are people. They respond to incentives just like consumers and business owners do. This idea changes how we understand everything from budgets to bailouts.

People, Not Angels

People in government are not self-sacrificing angels. They're humans. Because of this, we need to apply the same logic to government that we apply to everyone else and keep in mind:

- **Politicians want to stay in office.** They're rewarded for making promises and spending money in ways that secure votes, not necessarily in ways that create long-term prosperity.

- **Bureaucrats want more resources.** Agencies are rewarded for expanding their budgets, increasing staff, and regulating more things, not for becoming more efficient.

- **Voters are rational, but don't have all the information they may need.** Most citizens don't have time to research every policy or candidate. That's not laziness. It's a reasonable response to the low likelihood of their vote changing the outcome and the fact that there may be other more time-sensitive demands on their plate.

In this system, **each parties' behavior makes sense, but the outcomes often don't.**

Incentives in the Wrong Places

When private businesses serve customers poorly, they lose money. But in government, there's no equivalent feedback loop. The incentives don't always reward serving the public. They reward expanding power, budgets, and influence.

A few examples:

- **Politicians** propose popular programs, even if they're unaffordable, because the costs can be delayed while the (perceived) benefits are immediate.

- **Bureaucrats** rarely shrink their own departments. Why would they? Larger agencies mean more prestige, more funding, and more job security.

- **Lobbyists** seek favors from politicians and bureaucrats for their industries because the benefits are concentrated on their clients, while the costs are spread across millions of taxpayers who may never notice.

This isn't necessarily corruption, it's understandable behavior based on how the system is designed.

Why "Government Failure" Happens

Well-intentioned policies can fail. Not because of bad people, but because of bad incentives, knowledge, or both.

When policies are made through the political process:

- **Short-term optics can beat long-term planning.**

- **Symbolic victories can beat real solutions.**

- **Winners are chosen based on promises, not value creation.**

For instance, a politician might support giving taxpayer money to a specific industry not because it's good policy, but because that industry is located in a district they need to win or that maybe (likely) funds their campaign.

The result? Policies that look good on paper or at press conferences, but backfire in practice.

The Trouble With Benevolent Planning

Markets are messy, but they align incentives. Customers reward businesses that serve them well. Investors fund companies that manage uncertainty and deliver value.

Governments, by contrast, operate without prices, profit, or loss. Without those signals, planners must guess what people want. They understandably can, and do, guess wrong.

That's not a moral failing. It's both an **information problem** and a **motivation problem**.

No one becomes all-knowing or perfectly self-sacrificing just by winning an election or getting hired at a regulatory agency.

A Realistic View

Economics doesn't argue that governments can't do anything right. It simply insists we need to **build systems that account for how humans are, not how we wish they were**.

That means:

- **Aligning incentives.** For example, giving schools more autonomy while tying funding to what parents value, like performance, not how well they fill out forms.

- **Decentralizing decisions.** Local governments are often more accountable because they're closer to the people they affect.

- **Adding transparency.** Citizens need tools to see how money is spent and who benefits.

Like we discussed in Ch. 37, Good governance doesn't reliably come from simply finding better people. It often comes from better rules. We sometimes create rules based on the hope that we will get the brightest and best to be in charge. Ideally, we want the best and the brightest to do the most good possible once they are in office. But, at the same time, we very likely don't want a system where the best people can do the most good if that system also can allow the worst people to do the most bad.

We need rules where the worst people do the least harm because the people who end up in charge aren't always good.

One quick point. Neither the market nor the government is filled with angels. Market actors also face their own incentive problems. They can lie, cheat, mislead, and steal too. But, profit and loss within the market provide an important, although imperfect, correction mechanism that politics lacks.

The Bottom Line

Government actors are not above self-interest. Recognizing this isn't cynical, it's honest. Economics helps us understand why it's important to stop building for angels to be in charge and start designing systems that work for real people, with real incentives.

Chapter Forty-Two

We Grow When Anyone Can Compete

One Takeaway

Competition isn't about how many producers there are. It's about whether new ones are free to challenge them.

Monopoly and the Role of Competition

When people hear the word **monopoly**, they tend to picture a villainous company with total control. They envision someone choosing to set high prices, lowering their quality, and getting rich at everyone else's expense. But that image oversimplifies how markets work.

Here's an important idea: what matters most isn't whether there's more than one producer. **What matters most is whether others are free to compete.**

What Do We Mean By Monopoly?

Each of us is the only source of our own labor and ideas. Does that mean we are monopolists? No. Not in any way that matters. Just because we're the only provider of one specific type of good doesn't make us a threat to **competition.** So, the idea of monopoly isn't about being the only producer. Instead, historically, it was defined by a much larger issue: **protection.**

Protection, in this case, means **legal barriers to entry.** Sometimes people see things like high start up costs, geography, or control of specific resources as barriers. These barriers make competition harder, and in some cases they can keep competitors out for a long time. But they don't make competition permanently impossible the way legal protection does. Technology, innovation, and changing demand can eventually overcome even the highest natural barriers. Legal barriers can't be overcome by a better product.

Competition is most threatened when a producer is legally protected from new competitors.

When **a government-granted advantage** is given to a producer it can prevent others from entering the market. That's when consumers lose.

Why Government-Created Monopolies Hurt

When the government steps in and shields a business from competition, the trade-offs tend to work against consumers:

- **Innovation slows.** With no challengers, there's no pressure to improve.

- **Prices rise and quality drops.** Consumers have nowhere else to go.

- **Resources get misallocated.** Instead of chasing consumer wants, producers chase compliance, favors, or subsidies.

When you don't have to win customers, you stop making customers your highest priority.

Competition Is a Process, Not a Scorecard

The market isn't about how many firms exist right now. It's about whether entrepreneurs are **free to enter** when they see an opportunity.

Competition is a **process of discovery**. It's what happens when someone sees a better way to serve customers and decides to act. That pressure keeps even a lone producer honest to an extent, so long as others are free to challenge them.

Legal barriers can kill this process. When rules block new entrants—through licenses, zoning laws, or exclusive contracts—the process of competition breaks down, even if only one more firm was ever trying to enter.

Are Monopoly Laws Always Helpful?

Many people assume **antitrust laws** are the natural answer to monopoly power. And sometimes they've addressed real abuses. Sometimes they have broken up arrangements that blocked competitors and harmed consumers.

But antitrust laws come with their own trade-offs, and those are worth understanding.

Regulatory costs don't fall evenly. Large firms can afford teams of lawyers to navigate antitrust compliance. Smaller competitors and new entrants often can't. The rules meant to keep markets open can quietly raise the cost of entering them.

The line between dominance and excellence isn't always clear. A company might hold a large market share not because it blocked competitors, but because it built something consumers prefer. Penalizing that outcome can discourage the very innovation competition is supposed to reward.

Legal battles consume resources. When companies spend years and millions defending their position in court, that's time and money not spent improving products or serving customers. The process itself can become a competitive weapon that rivals may use to help win in the market.

None of this means antitrust law is useless. It means we should evaluate it the same way we evaluate any intervention: by asking whether it's actually increasing competition or just increasing complexity. **More rules don't automatically mean more challengers. Sometimes they mean fewer.**

A Story of Two Bakeries

Imagine a small town with one bakery. It's not a monopoly in any harmful sense. If the bakery raises prices or lowers quality, someone else is free to start a competing bakery.

Now imagine the town council passes a law saying no one else can open a bakery. That's basically giving the bakery permission to underperform. The bakery raises prices. Consumers have no other choice. Service declines. And customers are stuck.

The lesson? It's not about how many bakers exist. It's about whether someone new *could* bake a better loaf.

The Bottom Line

Competition isn't a number; it's a check on inefficient behavior. A lone firm in an open market still faces some form of discipline, because someone can always build a better mousetrap. Dangerous monopolies are formed when laws prevent challengers from entering. If you want better service, lower prices, and more innovation, the best policy is simple: don't block the next competitor.

Chapter Forty-Three

We Need Honest Money

One Takeaway

Central banks attempt to stabilize the economy, but by overriding market signals, they can cause the very instability they try to stop.

Two Grocery Trips

In 2020, you could fill a grocery cart for about $150. By 2026, that same cart cost closer to $200. Nothing about the food changed. The eggs are the same eggs. The bread is the same bread. But somewhere between those two trips, something happened to your **money.**

Most people have blamed the grocery store. Some have blamed supply chains. Some have blamed greedy corporations. But here's the question worth asking: what if the problem wasn't with the prices at all? What if the problem was with the money?

What Sits at the Center of It All

Money is the quiet infrastructure of every exchange. It connects buyers to sellers, borrowers to lenders, and savers to investors. But in most modern economies, one institution sits at the center of this system: a central bank.

Central banks, like the Federal Reserve in the United States, are tasked with managing the monetary system. Their responsibilities tend to include:

- Having a monopoly on issuing the currency everyone must accept.
- Regulating banks.
- Adjusting the cost of borrowing money for financial institutions.
- Being the lender of last resort for distressed financial institutions.

In theory, they attempt to bring stability to the monetary system.

But think about what that means. One institution decides how much money exists. One institution sets the price of borrowing. One institution signals to every business, family, and investor in the country whether now is the time to spend or save, expand or hold back.

That's an enormous amount of power concentrated in one place. And if those decisions are wrong, the consequences don't stay in Washington. They show up in your grocery cart.

How Inflation Works

Most people think of inflation as rising prices. That is one part of inflation. Inflation starts with an increase in the supply of money and credit. Rising prices are the result.

Not all rising prices are inflation. Prices can rise because of a drought that destroys crops or a spike in demand for a popular product. Those are real changes in supply and demand of specific goods. Inflation is different. Inflation is what happens when more money is created without a corresponding increase in goods and services. Inflation isn't about specific or relative prices. It's about the general price level across many goods.

Inflation most often enters the economy through three channels:

- Central banks injecting new money
- Governments borrowing and spending money they don't have
- Banks expanding credit

More dollars chase the same goods, so prices rise. But they don't all rise at once, and they don't all rise evenly.

Why It Doesn't Hit Everyone the Same Way

Imagine pouring dye into a pool. It doesn't spread evenly. The color is strongest near the source and fades as it moves outward.

That's how new money works. The first people to receive it (banks, large investors, government contractors) spend it before prices have adjusted. They get full purchasing power. By the time that money reaches wage earners, retirees, and savers, prices have already risen. Their dollars buy less.

This isn't just an inconvenience. It's a hidden redistribution. If a government raised taxes to take 25% of everyone's cash, people would notice. But if inflation quietly cuts your money's purchasing power by 25%, most people just blame the grocery store.

The Traffic Light Problem

Here's a way to see the bigger picture. Imagine a traffic light system where the lights change based on what traffic engineers think traffic *should* be, rather than responding to actual traffic flow. Sometimes it works fine. Other times you get green lights when no one's there and red lights when traffic is backed up for miles.

Now imagine this system controls every intersection in the country, and you can't install better traffic sensors.

That's what central banking does to money when they expand the money supply through credit expansions, issuing new money, or influencing interest rates. It can override the real signals that come from millions of people saving, spending, and borrowing based on their own lives with centralized guesses about what the economy needs. When those guesses are right, things feel smooth. When they're wrong, the whole system feels the impact.

Interest rates or credit issuances that don't reflect real savings mislead businesses into projects that can't be sustained. Expanded money supplies erode the value of what people have already earned. And bailouts for failing institutions teach the biggest players that they can take oversized risks because someone else will cover the losses.

The Bottom Line

Central banks promise stability, but by overriding the signals that coordinate millions of decisions, they risk delivering the opposite. Money works best when it tells the truth. When interest rates reflect real savings, businesses make better plans. When money holds its value, families can plan for the future. When the rules are stable, people can cooperate with confidence. Honest money matters not just for economic efficiency, but for fairness.

Chapter Forty-Four

We Can Crash When Cheap Money Lies

One Takeaway

When interest rates are kept lower than they should be, it sends false signals to entrepreneurs and leads to unsustainable booms followed by painful busts.

The Developer's Dilemma

Back in 2005, real estate developers in Las Vegas looked at the numbers and saw opportunity everywhere. Interest rates were low. Credit was easy to get. Housing prices had climbed every year for a decade. Dozens of developers borrowed millions to build new subdivisions on the edge of the town.

By 2007, the homes were built. But the buyers never showed up. Not because the homes were bad. Not because Vegas stopped growing. But because the borrowing and credit that made all of it possible was built on signals that weren't real.

Interest rates weren't low because Americans were saving more and banks had extra capital to lend. They were low because the Federal Reserve had pushed them there, in addition to ratings policy changes and a decrease in foreign investment.

When rates adjusted, the easy credit disappeared. Buyers couldn't get loans. Developers couldn't sell homes. Entire neighborhoods sat empty. The developer didn't make a reckless bet. He made a reasonable bet based on information that turned out to be false.

Now multiply that story by thousands of developers, in dozens of cities, across several industries and you start to see how an economy can boom and bust all at once.

Why Busts Hit Everything at the Same Time

We've been taught to think of recessions as a basic part of the economy. "What goes up must come down." But that's worth questioning. In a normal market, some industries grow while others shrink. That's expected. Consumers' wants change, technologies evolve, and seasons shift. But a bust that hits the whole economy at once? That's a sign something deeper went wrong.

What's the one thing that ties every industry together? **Money and credit.** If those are distorted, the problem doesn't stay in one place. It spreads everywhere.

What Interest Rates Are Supposed to Tell Us

Interest rates are more than the cost of a loan. They're a signal about time.

When people are saving more, there's generally more money available to lend. Interest rates tend to fall, telling entrepreneurs: "Go ahead and use credit for longer-term projects. Consumer demand will be there when you need it."

When people are spending more, less money is available. Rates tend to rise, telling entrepreneurs: "Now might not be the time for long-term bets."

In a healthy economy, interest rates coordinate what producers are building today with what consumers will want tomorrow.

What Happens When That Signal Is Faked?

When central banks push interest rates below where the market would set them, they send a message that isn't true: "People are saving. Long-term projects are safe bets."

Entrepreneurs see that signal and respond. They launch big, ambitious projects — new subdivisions, commercial towers, factory expansions — that feel justified by the low cost of borrowing. For a while, everything looks great. Businesses expand. Stock prices climb. Wages and hiring pick up.

But under the surface, the growth is hollow. The projects being built don't match what consumers actually want or can afford. The savings to support all that investment were never really there. Economists have a word for this: **malinvestment**. Not too much investment, but investment in the wrong things, guided by the wrong signals.

When Reality Shows Up

Eventually, the gap between what was built and what people actually want becomes impossible to ignore. Projects stall when demand doesn't materialize. Borrowers struggle to repay debts taken on during the boom. Resources locked into unsustainable ventures have to be freed and redirected to where they're actually needed.

That's the bust. It's painful. But it's also the economy correcting itself clearing out the mismatches so resources can find their way to better uses.

The Farmer and the False Forecast

Here's another way to see it. Imagine a farmer hears a weather forecast predicting record-breaking rainfall this year. Excited, he plants a water-hungry crop across every acre he owns.

For a few weeks, the fields look promising. But the rain never comes. The crops fail. The investment made perfect sense based on the forecast. The problem was the forecast was wrong.

That's what artificially low interest rates and easy credit do. They tell entrepreneurs the economic equivalent of "it's going to rain." Entrepreneurs "plant" accordingly. When the rain doesn't come, when the savings and ability to pay aren't actually there, the crops fail.

What This Means

The business cycle isn't some natural rhythm of the market process. It's what happens when the signals that coordinate millions of decisions get overridden.

When interest rates reflect real saving and spending, entrepreneurs can plan with less uncertainty. When they don't, even smart, careful people end up building the wrong things at the wrong time.

The bust isn't a disease that needs more intervention to be cured. It's the painful process of getting the diagnosis right and starting to heal.

The Bottom Line

The cause of economy-wide boom and bust cycle is bad information. When interest rates are manipulated, they stop reflecting existing conditions. Entrepreneurs then respond to signals that aren't real, and the economy pays for it later. The best way to avoid the cycle isn't better management of the boom. It's letting interest rates tell the truth in the first place.

Chapter Forty-Five

We Often Protect Producers At The Expense Of Consumers

One Takeaway

Regulations that try to protect consumers from harm can end up protecting producers from competition.

Rules Can Go Rogue

When people propose new laws or regulations for businesses to follow, the story always sounds the same. "We must protect the public, ensure fairness, and prevent abuse."

It's easy to support. Who doesn't want protection, fairness, or freedom from abuse? Clean air, safe food, and honest businesses are without a doubt good things.

But here's the harder truth: **regulation doesn't stay where it starts.** What begins as an attempt to **protect consumers** can evolve into **protecting producers.** It can shield businesses from competition instead of shielding consumers from harm.

Regulation Usually Starts With Genuine Concern

Most regulations begin with genuine concern. A product harms customers. A scandal sparks outrage. A problem feels like it needs a solution, and a rule seems like the obvious answer.

So, lawmakers form a new agency. Administrators write new standards. Bureaucrats put new approvals, inspections, and permits in place.

But the moment a rule is created, a new incentive emerges: **Who gets to influence how it works now that it exists?**

How Producers Take Control

Producers, trade groups, and industry associations, have a lot at stake in how regulation is written and enforced. Unlike individual consumers, they have the resources, time, and coordination to pay attention. They hire lobbyists, and they show up to every meeting.

This constant presence can cause rules to shift:

- A licensing law meant to ensure quality starts requiring expensive programs that only large companies can afford.

- Safety regulations begin mandating equipment that happens to be produced by a small number of approved vendors.

- Processes become so complex that only firms with full-time legal teams can make sense of them.

Regulations that were meant to protect the public start protecting the powerful instead.

When regulation makes it harder for new businesses to enter a market, it's not protecting consumers. It's protecting existing businesses.

Examples You May Recognize

Taxi medallions: Local governments created these to manage traffic and ensure safety. They are a barrier to entry and limit who can compete. They lead to less supply and higher prices as a result.

Occupational licensing: Governments can require licenses for certain jobs not because of risk to the public, but because established professionals want to limit competition.

Food safety rules: Sometimes written so narrowly that small farmers or producers can't comply, even if their practices are safer and more transparent than industrial alternatives.

Consumers don't always benefit from these rules as much as producers do.

Regulation as a Competitive Strategy

Here's what's really going on: **established businesses can use regulation as a weapon against their rivals.**

A large firm might support stricter environmental rules because it already has the resources to comply. The business may know their smaller competitors don't have the funds to make the changes fast enough.

An industry association might lobby for mandatory certifications, knowing it can train its members to pass them while leaving outsiders behind.

Even well-meaning laws can be subtly rewritten over time to entrench those already at the top. Economists call this behavior **regulatory capture.**

Why It's Hard to Reverse

Once a regulation shifts toward producer protection, it's hard to reverse.

- The rules are already in place.

- Those benefiting are organized.
- The costs are spread across millions of people who rarely notice.

Consumers rarely lobby to repeal a license requirement. But producers have the money and people to fight hard to keep it. Especially if it locks in their advantage.

This is why regulation tends to expand, even if it doesn't work that well. The people who benefit most are the ones best positioned to defend it.

What Can Work Better

Regulation doesn't always have to come from the government. Markets provide ways to regulate businesses as a result of different groups working together pursuing their own goals.

Insurance companies assess risk and adjust pricing. They can create strong incentives for businesses to maintain safe practices to keep premiums low.

Independent quality assurance groups set standards and certifications that consumers trust. Companies compete to earn these certifications because consumers value them.

Industry self-regulation often sets higher standards than the government. Professional groups understand their industries better and are incentivized to maintain credibility.

These **market based accountability** mechanisms can fail too. None of them are perfect. But, the question is which system fails less catastrophically and corrects faster. The market has an incentive to adapt. When businesses know they'll pay for harm they cause, they have a powerful incentive to maintain safety and quality. This can disappear when there's a possibility for the laws to change in their favor.

The Bottom Line

Even when regulation starts with good intentions, it can be used as a weapon against competitors by those with the most to gain. Consumers rarely win from this. But competitors, lobbyists, and insiders often do. To truly protect the public, regulations should rely on rules that hold businesses accountable for harm, and less on complex regulations that just protect incumbents.

Chapter Forty-Six

We Benefit When We Trade Across Borders

One Takeaway

International trade works the same way as any other voluntary exchange. Both sides benefit, even when one country is "better" at producing everything.

Why Trade Scares People

When a factory closes and jobs move overseas, it's natural to blame foreign competition.

When imports flood the market, it feels like other countries are "taking advantage" of us.

When politicians promise to "bring jobs back," it sounds like they're fighting for workers.

But this view misses something important. **Trade isn't war. It's cooperation.** Just like trade between individuals, international trade makes everyone involved better off.

The Same Logic, Bigger Scale

Everything that is beneficial about exchange between people applies to countries, too.

When you trade with your neighbor, you both benefit because you each give up something you value less to get something you value more. The same thing happens when Americans buy coffee from Colombia or when Germans buy software from Silicon Valley.

Countries don't trade. People do.

Productiveland and Struggleton

Here's where it gets interesting. **Even if one country is better at producing everything, trade still benefits both countries.**

Imagine two countries, Productiveland and Struggleton. Productiveland can make all items more efficiently than Struggleton. You might think, "Why would Productiveland ever trade with Struggleton?"

The answer lies in opportunity cost. Even though Productiveland is better at making all products, it has to choose how to use its limited resources. If Productiveland focuses on mostly computers (where its advantage is biggest) and Struggleton focuses on clothing (where its disadvantage is smallest), both countries can end up with more of both products.

Struggleton may never buy as much from Productiveland as Productiveland buys from Struggleton. But, that's because Struggleton doesn't need as many computers as Productiveland needs clothes. At least not yet.

The goal is not to have an equal balance of trade. **The goal is to have the cheapest trade possible to allow for the most exchange possible.** That way both parties benefit the most.

Why Jobs Arguments Miss the Point

Critics of trade tend to focus on the jobs lost in some industries. These losses are real and painful. But they miss the other side of the equation:

- **Consumers benefit** from lower prices and better products. A family that saves $2,000 a year on clothing and electronics has $2,000 more to spend on other things. This creates demand and jobs elsewhere.

- **Export industries grow.** When other countries buy our products, that creates jobs here. That extra demand leads to growth.

- **Resources shift to better uses.** We free up workers and capital for industries where we have an advantage when we stop making products that others can make more efficiently.

The job losses are visible and concentrated. The job gains are spread out and harder to see. But both are real.

What About "Unfair" Competition?

Sometimes people argue that trade is only fair if wages and working conditions are similar across countries. But this misses why trade happens in the first place.

Countries trade because they're different. They have different resources, different skills, and different costs. A country with lower wages usually has lower productivity, too. When they specialize in labor-heavy products, it gives them the ability to build skills and capital that raise wages over time.

Blocking this process doesn't help foreign workers. It traps them in poverty. And it doesn't help domestic workers either. It forces them to pay higher prices for goods they could get more cheaply through trade.

The Real Costs of Protection

When governments try to "protect" domestic industries with tariffs or quotas, they create several problems:

- **Consumers pay more.** Tariffs are taxes on imports, and those taxes get passed on as higher prices.

- **Efficiency falls.** Protected industries have less incentive to innovate and improve.

- **Retaliation happens.** Other countries respond with their own trade barriers, hurting our exporters.

The result? We get less stuff, at higher prices, produced less efficiently. That "protection" leads to everyone paying more so that one group doesn't have to adapt.

This pattern reveals something important about how politics shapes economics. **Political incentives and promises can often override economic logic.**

What This Means for Policy

Good trade policy focuses on **reducing barriers**, not raising them. This means:

- **Lower tariffs** that let consumers choose based on value, not artificial price differences.

- **Fewer regulations** that make it harder for our exporters to compete globally.

- **Better systems** that make it easy for workers to adapt when industries change, rather than trying to freeze industries in place.

The Bottom Line

International trade doesn't destroy jobs, it changes them. Some industries shrink while others grow. Some workers need to retrain while others see new opportunities. Reducing barriers for workers to change industries is key. That transition can be difficult, but blocking trade doesn't stop the need for change. It just makes everyone poorer in the process.

Chapter Forty-Seven

Short Answer: We Get Unintended Consequences From Good Intentions

When the City Tried to Help Elena's Employees

The city council, the same one that wanted to plan coffee shop locations, passes a new law. Every coffee shop with more than five full time employees must provide health insurance or pay an additional fee to the city. The intention is good: make sure workers like Elena's baristas have healthcare coverage.

But you now have a way to think past the stated intention. And it changes what you see.

Who responds, and how? Elena has six employees. She can't absorb the insurance cost. Her margins are thin. She runs the numbers and faces three options: raise prices, cut a position, or reduce some employee hours to stay under the threshold. She raises her latte price by seventy-five cents and cuts one full-time shift. The large chain down the street absorbs the cost easily. They have scale Elena doesn't. The law was meant to help workers. It's making it harder for the smallest employers to compete.

Who gets hurt that nobody's talking about? The baristas who kept their jobs get coverage. That's the visible outcome; the one the council member puts in a press release. But the sixth employee lost her full-time status. A college student who applied last week also didn't get hired because Elena decides five employees is her new ceiling. And customers who now pay $6.75 instead of $6 come less often, which means less revenue and Elena is further from being able to afford that sixth employee. These costs are invisible. They don't show up at the press conference.

Does this solve the problem or move it? The policy was supposed to help workers afford healthcare. But if one worker loses her job and another doesn't get hired, the problem didn't disappear. It moved. It went from "workers without insurance" to "workers without shifts."

Would you support this if the other party proposed it? Strip the politics away from the policy. A regulation that raises costs on small businesses, benefits large chains that can absorb the expense, and reduces employment for the workers it claims to help doesn't magically become good because you're on the team of whoever proposed it. The economics are the same regardless of who signed the bill.

The lesson isn't that Elena's employees don't deserve healthcare. It's that achieving that goal requires understanding how people like Elena actually respond to the rules we set. She's not heartless. She's doing math. And the math doesn't change because the intention behind the law is compassionate.

Good intentions matter. But good intentions without good understanding produce the opposite of what we want. The people who pay for that gap are usually the ones the policy was supposed to help.

Can Markets Be Moral?

We all (hopefully) also care about fairness, justice, and what kind of society we want to live in. Can markets be moral? How should we think about inequality? What's the relationship between economic freedom and human flourishing? These aren't just philosophical questions. They're questions about how we want to live together.

Chapter Forty-Eight

We Need Ethics And Economics To Build A Better World

One Takeaway

Ethical progress requires economic understanding. Good intentions can't overcome bad incentives or broken systems.

Two Sides of the Same Coin

Economics and ethics might seem like two separate worlds. One seems to be focused on numbers and systems, the other on right and wrong. But in the real world, they're inseparable.

Every economic action has ethical implications. Every ethical rule has economic consequences.

You can't separate how people behave from what people believe.

Why Economics Needs Ethics

At its core, economics studies human action. But people don't act in a vacuum. We act with others. **We cooperate, compete, trade, produce, and consume in a world surrounded by others.** We interact under rules, with expectations, in systems that reward some behaviors and punish others.

And that's where ethics enters the picture.

- **Institutions reflect our values.** Property rights, contract law, and rules about fraud or theft all emerge from moral norms.

- **Exchange assumes consent.** Markets don't work without voluntary agreement, without some foundation of mutual respect.

- **Consequences matter.** Economic systems impact well-being, opportunity, and justice. Ignoring that fact leaves us blind to the full picture.

Ethics answers questions related to how we should treat and interact with each other. Economics helps us understand how those ethical goals can best be achieved given the features of our world.

Why Ethics Needs Economics

Ethics deals with intentions. But as we've discussed, **good intentions aren't enough to ensure good results follow.** Policies that aim to help can backfire. That's where economics steps in by asking: "do the tools you're using actually work?"

Economics focuses on:

- **Means, not ends.** It doesn't decide what your goals should be. It just tests whether the path you've chosen gets you there.

- **Consequences, not slogans.** It looks at what really happens, not what we wish would happen.

You can believe in fairness, and still see that minimum wage laws, for example, can hurt the least experienced workers. We all wish that helping others was as easy as passing a law, but the world is much more complicated than that.

If we care about those who are disadvantaged, then it's only appropriate for us to support programs and ideas that actually help, rather than simply making a promise to help.

The lesson? **Ethics without economics can become well-intentioned failure.**

When Good Intentions Go Wrong

Consider a city that wants to help low-income families afford housing. The ethical goal is admirable. But if the solution is rent control, the economic consequences may hurt the very people the policy aimed to help:

- Landlords can stop maintaining buildings if it costs them too much to repair

- New housing construction can slow if the returns are capped

- Existing tenants can't move without losing their cheap rent

- Housing shortages worsen over time

The intention was ethical. The outcome was harmful. Understanding economics doesn't change the moral goal. It helps us find tools that achieve it.

The goal is not to support every idea that claims to help others. The goal is to support the ideas that actually do help others. The problem we face is markets can't fix every problem for every person immediately. But that shouldn't be the standard for evaluation because governments can't do that either.

The question is: which one leads to outcomes that help for longer than a short while?

Policy is Where They Collide

This is why policy discussions get so heated. People with the same ethical goals end up disagreeing about the best methods to achieve them.

- **Intentions vs. Outcomes:** A policy can aim to help and still hurt. It can promise justice and still cause harm.
- **Trade-offs, Not Solutions:** Every action has a cost. Every fix creates new frictions. Pretending otherwise leads to failure. Our option set is better or worse situations rather than perfect or disastrous.
- **Respecting Choice:** Because value is personal, ethical systems that respect individual choice and voluntary action tend to work best, especially when paired with institutions that hold people accountable.

If you want to do good in the world, you have to start with respecting and understanding how humans are wired, rather than how you wish they were.

The Bottom Line

Ethics without economics is blind, and economics without ethics is empty. To build a better society, we need both. The most ethical path forward is one that respects freedom, learns from feedback, and avoids causing harm, even when trying to help.

Chapter Forty-Nine

We Cooperate Because We Choose To

One Takeaway

Markets are moral not because they're perfect, but because they are based on choice, reward cooperation, and reveal what works.

The Moral Power of Voluntary Exchange

Not only is the market process efficient. It's also ethical. At their foundation lies a simple but powerful principle: **no one forces anyone to trade.**

When I voluntarily pay you to achieve something that I want, I end up benefiting you by pursuing what I want.

Every exchange happens because both people believe they'll be better off. That's not just good economics. It's good ethics.

Three Pillars of Market Morality

- **Voluntary Exchange:** Each person only agrees to trade if they believe they're better off. No force. Just mutual benefit.

- **Personal Value:** People define value for themselves. You don't have to justify your preferences to anyone else. Your choices reflect your goals, not someone else's idea of what's good for you.

- **Property Rights:** Ownership gives people the incentive to care for, improve, and exchange resources productively. When you own something, you have reason to maintain it and use it wisely.

Markets create cooperation between strangers. They align individual freedom with mutual benefit. They turn self-interest into service to others.

Markets Work With Human Nature, Not Against It

Here's the crucial insight: markets work best when people do act with moral intentions. But that's true of any system. **The trouble is, we can't force people to have moral intentions.**

If we could rely on everyone to be perfectly moral, cooperation would be easy. **But since none of us are angels, we need a system that gives even selfish people strong reasons to benefit others.**

That's exactly what markets do. By seeking to make our own lives better through voluntary trade, we often benefit others' lives more than we could through voluntary or forced charity alone. A baker who just wants to make money still has to bake good bread for others to succeed. A software developer who only cares about profit still has to solve real problems for users.

Where Markets Face Ethical Challenges

Markets aren't utopias. They reflect the world as it is—imperfect, dynamic, and sometimes unfair. But they give us a framework to understand trade-offs:

- **Inequality:** People differ in skills, timing, effort, and luck. That creates uneven outcomes. The ethical challenge isn't to enforce sameness, but instead to remove barriers and open opportunity.

- **Spillover Damages:** Some actions affect others indirectly (like pollution). These effects are real. But they're best addressed through clear property rights and enforceable rules, not top-down mandates.

- **Imperfect Choices:** Sometimes people face difficult trade-offs with no perfect options. The goal isn't to eliminate hard choices (which is impossible). The goal is to expand the range of choices available through competition, opportunity, and innovation.

In these situations, we have two general approaches. One is to ban certain actions or make them illegal. The other, more economic approach, is to ask: **"What incentives in our system created this situation, and can we change them to encourage better outcomes?"**

Why Voluntary Matters

The key word is voluntary. When people are **free to choose**, they reveal what they value. When they're forced to comply, we learn nothing about their real preferences, and they can end up worse off.

When a voluntary transaction occurs, it means both people expected to benefit. A forced transfer means someone with power decided what was best for someone without it. Sometimes that decision reflects genuine shared values. But the further a decision moves from individual consent, the harder it becomes to know whether it's truly serving the people it claims to help.

That's why voluntary exchange carries a moral weight that forced exchange doesn't. Cooperation that people choose tells us something real about what they value. Cooperation that people are compelled into might produce good outcomes, but it also might not. We often won't know until the consequences arrive. **The best outcomes come from systems that rely on choice wherever possible, and resort to collective decisions with humility about how much the decision-makers actually know.**

Unintended Results Matter

Ethics usually focuses on intentions, but economics focuses on results. This creates an interesting paradox: markets can unintentionally benefit society more than intentional, morally justified, but forced actions.

A business owner motivated purely by profit might create more jobs, serve more customers, and contribute more to community prosperity than someone with perfect intentions but poor understanding of how to actually help others.

This doesn't mean intentions don't matter. It means that good intentions without good results aren't enough. That systems matter more than individual virtue.

The Bottom Line

Markets are moral because they're built on choice, consent, and mutual benefit. They work with human nature rather than against it, channeling self-interest toward serving others. They're not perfect, but they provide a framework for people to cooperate without being forced. In an imperfect world populated by imperfect people, systems that honor individual choice while encouraging service to others offer the best path toward both prosperity and human dignity.

Chapter Fifty

We Can't End Inequality, But We Can Stop Picking Favorites

One Takeaway

Inequality can be harmful, however what matters is whether it comes from outcompeting or from rigging the rules to serve yourself.

Inequality is Everywhere

No two people are the same. We have different skills, priorities, and luck. So, it's no surprise that we don't all end up with the same results. **Inequality is an inescapable feature of life.**

Both societies with markets and good institutions and societies with bad markets and institutions have inequality. The question is, which does better compared to the alternative? The results overwhelmingly favor those with markets held together by good institutions.

A widening gap in wealth within a country can harm overall prosperity. The question isn't whether inequality exists. It's understanding why specific inequalities exist so we can do something about the ones that matter.

What Causes Inequality

Market inequality arises for natural reasons:

- **Different Skills and Preferences:** People make different choices. Some work longer hours, take more chances, or prioritize family over career.

- **Entrepreneurial Success:** Some create products people want and are rewarded for it.

- **Savings and Investment:** People who delay consumption and reinvest earnings tend to build wealth over time.

And yes, some wealth is inherited. That's a real advantage. But even inherited wealth can be quickly disciplined by markets over time. Families that don't continue creating value tend to lose it within a few generations. Political advantages, by contrast, can be locked in indefinitely. The question isn't whether starting points are unequal. They always will be. The question is whether the system rewards continued value creation or allows advantages to be protected through favoritism.

Market Inequality vs. Political Inequality

Not all inequality is the same. There's a distinct difference between market inequality and political inequality.

Market Inequality happens when people serve others differently. It rewards value creation. Some people create more value for others and earn more as a result.

Political Inequality happens when people seek special treatment through the government. It rewards lobbying, favoritism, and manipulation.

This distinction matters. One reflects **voluntary exchange.** The other reflects **favoritism and control**.

A company that wins in the market because it serves customers better should be celebrated. But a company that wins because it lobbied for government payouts or blocked competitors through regulation is not creating value. It's capturing it.

One important point to make is that these two categories can blur in practice. Sometimes entrepreneurs can start focused on value creation and serving others and then over time begin to focus on seeking special treatment. This blurring makes it difficult to separate the effects of each. And that blurring is itself the problem.

Why Equal Outcomes Are Harder Than They Sound

Most of us want a fair society, and for good reason. But there's an important difference between equalizing opportunity and equalizing outcomes.

When we try to guarantee equal results, we often have to override the very processes that create opportunity in the first place. If the rewards for taking a chance, building something new, or investing years of effort can be redistributed after the fact, fewer people will take those chances. Not because they're selfish, but because incentives matter.

The goal shouldn't be to prevent anyone from getting ahead. It should be to prevent anyone from rigging the rules so that others can't.

What We Can Do Instead

We can reduce political inequality without trying to erase market differences:

- **Eliminate barriers to entry** so new competitors can rise.
- **End favoritism** by stopping subsidies, bailouts, and protections.
- **Decentralize power** so people can't rig the system from the top.

This encourages competition. Not everyone will win equally, but everyone can play under the same rules. With fair rules markets reward serving others rather than keeping them down. The more competitive the market the more success relies on making what consumers value for the lowest possible cost.

The Bottom Line

Inequality can be the result of both political and market forces. Inequality isn't always a problem. It's often the result of freedom and diversity. But **how** inequality arises matters. **Market inequality** rewards people for serving others. It reflects choice, not coercion. **Political inequality** rewards people for manipulating rules. It creates resentment and wastes resources. If we care about fairness, progress, and opportunity, we need to **target political favoritism, not success**.

Chapter Fifty-One

Short Answer: We Make Markets Moral Through Our Choices

Good Intentions Need Good Information

We've followed Elena's coffee shop from the savings that built it, through the policies that squeezed it, through the employee she lost to a well-meaning mandate. Now one final question: is economics just about people looking out for themselves? Does morality have anything to do with it?

It started with a conversation at the counter. Maria, one of Elena's regulars, asked a simple question one morning: "Where do your beans come from? Are they fair trade?"

Elena didn't have a good answer. She'd been buying from a regional distributor. She knew the beans were good quality, had reliable delivery, and were a fair price. But she'd never looked deeper than that. Maria's question stuck with her. If she was going to charge $6 for a latte, shouldn't she know whether the people who grew the beans were being treated well?

So, Elena started investigating the same way she'd researched equipment, locations, and suppliers when she built the shop. And what she found surprised her.

She looked into fair trade certification first. The label promised ethical sourcing, better prices for farmers, and sustainable practices. It sounded like exactly what Maria was asking for. But the costs were significant. Certified beans were more expensive, and the certification process itself required fees and paperwork that added to the price. Elena could make the switch, but it would mean raising prices again or cutting her already thin margins.

Then she met Carlos.

A roaster she trusted introduced her to Carlos, a coffee farmer from Guatemala. Carlos didn't participate in fair trade certification, even though his farming practices were more sustainable and his workers were paid better than many certified farms.

The certification costs were prohibitive. Fair trade required expensive inspections, paperwork, and compliance that Carlos couldn't afford. He was too small to navigate the bureaucracy, despite treating his workers and land better than some larger certified operations.

The guaranteed prices weren't always better. Fair trade offers a price floor, but when market prices rise above that floor, certified farmers can't always capture the higher prices due to contracts. Carlos sold directly to roasters who paid him based on quality, not certification.

And some large coffee growers gamed the system. They would meet minimum requirements while maximizing profits in ways that didn't necessarily help workers. Meanwhile, small farmers like Carlos were excluded from the premium market despite their practices.

Elena faced the same puzzle Maria's question had created, but now with better information. Which choice was more moral: buying certified beans that might not help the farmers she intended to support, or building a direct relationship with a farmer like Carlos and paying him a fair price based on quality, visiting when she could, and telling her customers exactly where their coffee came from?

She chose Carlos. Not because certification is worthless, but because she could see that the label and the outcome weren't the same thing. She started printing Carlos's farm name on her menu. She shared his story with customers who asked. Maria was the first to notice.

The certified label would have made Elena's customers feel ethical. Understanding how the system actually worked helped Elena *be* ethical. That's a meaningful difference.

Now here's what this means for you.

You face versions of Elena's dilemma constantly. You see a label, a certification, a brand promise. You have to decide whether it means what it claims. So, before you trust it, ask what you'd ask about any economic claim: how does this actually work? Who benefits, and does the benefit reach the people it's supposed to? Is there a simpler, more direct path between my values and the outcome I want?

These questions don't make you cynical. They make you effective. Elena moved from feeling good about her sourcing to understanding whether her sourcing was actually doing good.

What's The One Lesson To Take With You?

If you take just one thing from this book, it should be this: the world is full of trade-offs, and seeing them clearly is the first step toward making better choices. Thinking like an economist can help you cut through the noise and focus on what matters in your busy life.

Chapter Fifty-Two

We Must Think Past The First Step

One Takeaway

The most useful habit economics can give you is simple: when you see something happen, ask what happens next, and to whom.

Back to the Desert

We started this book in a sushi bar behind a 7/11 in Las Vegas, watching a razor clam crack open its shell. I asked a question then: what is *that* doing here?

By now, you know the answer. Not because someone explained the global seafood supply chain to you, but because you understand something deeper. Thousands of strangers cooperated across oceans and time zones. They didn't cooperate because anyone told them to. They did it because prices, incentives, and voluntary exchange connected people who would never meet into a system that delivered exactly what I didn't know I wanted.

You've seen that same system at work in something even more ordinary. A cup of coffee. You watched it go from a personal choice at the counter to a global supply chain coordinated without a plan. You saw what it took to build the shop that serves it. You saw what happens when well-meaning policies try to reshape it. You followed it all the way to a farm in Guatemala and asked whether the whole system is moral.

One cup of coffee. Every economic principle in this book. Economics isn't hiding in textbooks. It's sitting on your desk right now, waiting for you to see it.

The Broken Window

Remember the bakery window from earlier in this book? A kid breaks it. Someone shrugs and says, "Well, at least the window maker gets paid." And you now know what most people miss. The baker was going to buy an oven. That money is gone. The oven maker gets nothing. The bakery doesn't grow.

One visible benefit. A dozen invisible costs. Economic activity is not the same as economic progress.

That idea, looking past the first step to what's hidden underneath, is the single most useful habit this book has (hopefully) given you. And most of the world never does it. You don't have to be most of the world anymore.

If Economics Is So Useful, Why Isn't It Used More Often?

By now, you've seen how useful these ideas are. You've applied them to your morning routine, your decisions, your city's policies, your ethical choices. So, a natural question follows: if economics is this useful, why don't more people think this way?

The honest answer is that we're wired to look for certainty and markets rely on uncertainty.

A new restaurant opens in your neighborhood. The food is great. People line up. Six months later, it closes. Maybe the rent went up. Maybe the owner burned out. Maybe a better option opened across the street. It feels like a loss. And a natural thought follows: couldn't someone have prevented this?

That instinct — the desire for someone to be in charge, to prevent the mess, to guarantee the outcome — is one of the deepest reasons people overlook, or ignore, the ideas in this book. Not because they've studied economics and found it wanting. But because markets feel uncertain. **And uncertainty feels like a problem that ought to have a solution.**

Compare what markets produce to what a confident plan promises. Markets give you results that may be hard to see, slow to arrive, and unevenly distributed. A plan gives you a target, a timeline, and a "guarantee." The plan feels safer. It feels like someone is steering.

But you now know what most people don't. The signals that coordinate an economy — prices, profits, losses, incentives — don't come from a plan. They emerge from millions of people making decisions based on what they know and what they value. No planner has access to all of that information. No promise, assurance, or guarantee can substitute for the feedback that comes from people freely choosing. And every time we trade adaptability for the promise of certainty, we lose the very thing that makes progress possible.

The restaurant that closed wasn't a failure of the system. It was the system working. Resources moved from something that wasn't serving people well enough to something that might. That process is uncomfortable. But it's how economies learn. It's how Elena learned which five drinks to keep on her menu. It's how the farmer in Colombia learned which beans to plant. It's how you learned which coffee shop deserves your $6.

What You Now Carry With You

You don't have to love uncertainty. Nobody does. But you now understand something most people never grasp: **the messy, unpredictable process is how we find out what actually works.**

When someone offers a plan that guarantees an outcome, you'll ask:

what trade-offs are hidden? What signals are being overridden? What won't exist tomorrow because we chose control over adaptability today?

When you see a headline number on the nightly news, you won't just react. You'll read past it to the people and decisions underneath.

When you face a choice about money, time, risk, or policy, you'll ask what you're giving up, not just what you're getting.

And when you look at your morning coffee, you'll see something most people miss: a small miracle of cooperation, built on differences, sustained by signals, and made possible by the freedom of millions of strangers to choose for themselves.

The Bottom Line

I didn't write this book to give you all the answers. I wrote it to give you a better set of questions.

Economics is the most useful science most people never use. You're no longer most people.

Let's get busy.

Afterward: We're Finished, But You Aren't Done

My Sincerest Gratitude

Thank you for giving this book a chance.

My hope is, if you've made it this far, you now understand more about how the economy works than you did before.

This book is a beginning. I haven't addressed every criticism, argument, study, or debate in economic science. That wasn't my goal.

My goal was to build a foundation that's extremely important to have, even though it's insufficient to solve every problem in the world on its own.

The good news? You're too busy to solve every problem in the world. We all are. But that doesn't mean you're too busy to make a difference on the margin.

I didn't set out to help you master economics. I wanted to explain enough for you to think more clearly about the real world and make better decisions starting Monday (or whatever day tomorrow is).

No Citations?

Maybe you noticed that there weren't any citations or references throughout the book. This was on purpose. This wasn't out of disrespect or to claim these ideas as my own. To be clear: the vast majority of these ideas aren't mine. I didn't invent modern economics. I've relied heavily on economists much better than I am.

But the way I've presented these ideas is my own. And any errors are definitely my own.

I chose to exclude in-text citations and references because I wanted to keep the book short and clear. **Knowing an idea and knowing how to use it matters more than knowing who came up with it when you just want to start making better decisions right now** (which is what I assume your goal was when you chose to start reading).

If We Disagree

If you're thinking "this is complete nonsense," you won't hurt my feelings. I welcome disagreements.

If you find yourself disagreeing with any of the points or conclusions, I'd suggest two things:

1. **Keep reading.** I've listed additional books and articles in the Further Reading section. There's much more from much better economists out there waiting to be read.

2. **Reach out and let's talk.**

By releasing this book, I've opened myself up to criticism and feedback. I can handle whatever discussion you want to have. We don't have enough discussion of ideas in our current world. I honestly enjoy disagreements because they help us learn.

One thing I don't enjoy, however, is disagreeable people. So, if you reach out, let's cooperate rather than conflict.

The Real Goal

Economics isn't about being right or wrong. It's about thinking clearly about how the world works. If this book helped you do that a little better, then it succeeded.

Hopefully you're now one of the people who will take these ideas off the page and out into the world. I truly think the success of society depends on it.

Thanks for fitting this book into your busy schedule.

Acknowledgements

Many people were essential to the writing and publishing of this book. While I acknowledge everyone below, any and all errors within the book are my own.

First and foremost, all praise, glory, and honor belong to God the Father, God the Son Jesus Christ, and God The Holy Spirit. All good things come from God and without Him nothing is possible. "The Lord is my Shepard, there is nothing I lack." (Psalm 23:1)

To my amazing wife Amber Belt. First, you continue to put up with our house doubling as a small library. You knew this before you married me, so it's no surprise, but I am still grateful for you putting up with the weekly book deliveries. Second, your reading out loud of early drafts helped me spot errors, confusing statements, and places to add in humor. I am blessed to be your husband. Thank you for being with me on this journey.

To my mother Suzanne, my father Jerry, my stepfather Andreas, my father-in-law John, and my brother Steven. Each of you helped in some way while I was writing this book by reading early drafts, listening to my frustrations, or coming up with new ideas and people to share the work with. Thank you for your constant love and support. I wouldn't be here without all of you.

To my family, close friends, and colleagues who were willing to provide feedback, help promote, and push me further in this journey whenever I began to stall. Your time and talents each helped improve this book in some way and kept me motivated to finish. Special thanks to: David

Freeman, Spencer Freeman, Joseph Diedrich, John Restrepo, Dr. Shawn McCoy, John Tsarpalas, Geoff Lawrence, Eric Bihr, Anahit Baghshetsyan, Zachary Walkerlieb, Michael Huggins, Mary Huggins, Kalix Muangchoo, Paul Roberson, Benji Sloan, Connor Filley, Mike Blake, Hunter Hastings, Doug French, Alexander McCobin, and Averey O'Leary.

This book's original form was created when I was finishing grad school and on the launch team for Liberty.me in 2015. The goal at that time was to create an intro to economics course that got people to "cocktail party-level knowledge." Many people helped at the stage including Jeffrey Tucker, David and Reagan Luntz, Mike Reid, Patrick Hatten, and BK Marcus.

To every early subscriber of my Substack, EconomicsFor.com, where these chapters were first released and tested, thank you for your support and willingness to engage with me. Special thanks to Mark Monroe for being the first subscriber to pledge and support the platform. That vote of confidence was a huge boost of inspiration.

To the event organizers and audience attendees that I have had the honor of speaking in front of since 2015, thank you for your time, attention, and willingness to listen. Those presentations helped shape my communication abilities and sparked the idea to pick this project back up.

Further Reading, Listening, or Watching

Where to Go From Here

You just finished a book designed to give you the foundations in about five minutes per chapter. If any of the ideas sparked your curiosity, here are the best next steps.

If You Want Another Book Like This One

Hazlitt, Henry. ***Economics in One Lesson.*** The closest relative to the book you just read. Hazlitt takes one idea, look beyond the immediate effects (the conclusion you just read), and applies it to dozens of real-world policies. Short, clear, and timeless.

Read, Leonard E. "I, Pencil." A short essay that tells the story of how a simple pencil gets made, and why no single person on earth knows how to make one. You can read it in ten minutes and you'll never look at ordinary objects the same way. Available free online at the Foundation for Economic Education. This was the inspiration for the introduction.

If You're Curious About How People Act, Choose, and Cooperate

Heyne, Paul T., Peter J. Boettke, and David L. Prychitko. ***The Economic Way of Thinking.*** If you want a fuller treatment of the ideas in this book with more depth and examples, this is the best single volume. It reads like a textbook but thinks like a conversation. The closest thing to a complete economics education in one book.

Murphy, Robert, and Donald J. Boudreaux. ***Choice: Cooperation, Enterprise, and Human Action.*** A modern, readable presentation of the full framework behind the ideas in this book. More depth than what you've read here, but written for a general audience rather than academics.

Roberts, Russ. ***How Adam Smith Can Change Your Life.*** Not about economics in the way you'd expect. Roberts uses Adam Smith's lesser-known book on human nature to explore why people cooperate, what drives moral behavior, and how we navigate social life.

If You Want to Learn Why Good Intentions Can Backfire

Bastiat, Frédéric. ***Economic Sophisms and "What Is Seen and What Is Not Seen".*** The original source for the broken window story and dozens of other examples of how popular economic reasoning goes wrong. Written in the 1800s but it reads like it was written yesterday. Funny, sharp, and short.

Sowell, Thomas. ***Basic Economics.*** A comprehensive tour of how economies work and why well-meaning interventions often produce the opposite of what they intend. No graphs, no jargon, just clear thinking applied to real-world problems. Longer than this book but just as accessible. Written by one of the greatest economists living right now.

Friedman, Milton and Rose D. Friedman. *Free to Choose.* A Nobel Prize winning economist and his wife, who is also a great economist, walk through how markets serve people and how government policies often hurt the people they're designed to help. Originally a PBS television series, so the writing is built for a general audience.

If You Want More on Money, Prices, and Business Cycles

Murphy, Robert P. *Understanding Money Mechanics.* A clear, accessible guide to how money actually works. It covers where money comes from, how banks create credit, and why inflation hits some people harder than others. Starts simple and builds carefully.

Horwitz, Steven. *Austrian Economics: An Introduction.* If you're curious about the tradition behind many of the ideas in this book, this is the best short introduction. Horwitz explains the key concepts without assuming any background and connects them to real-world applications.

If You're Interested in Markets, Morality, and Rules

Storr, Virgil Henry, and Ginny Seung Choi. *Do Markets Corrupt Our Morals?* Tackles the question head-on with evidence and careful reasoning. If Part 9 of this book left you wanting more on whether markets make us better or worse people, start here.

Leeson, Peter T. *The Invisible Hook.* The economics of pirates. Seriously. Leeson shows how pirates created constitutions, insurance systems, and governance long before modern governments did. Entertaining and surprisingly relevant to how institutions emerge without central planning.

Boettke, Peter J., Stefanie Haeffele-Balch, and Virgil Henry Storr. ***Mainline Economics.*** Six Nobel Prize lectures from economists in the tradition this book draws from. If you want to hear the ideas at their source — from Hayek, Buchanan, Ostrom, and others — this is the most accessible collection.

If You Want to Watch or Listen

These books represent a starting point, not a finish line. Economics is a living discipline, and the best way to keep learning is to keep asking the questions this book taught you to ask. Beyond books, the organizations below produce articles, videos, podcasts, and educational content that will help you keep building on the ideas in this book. Most of it is free and designed for general audiences, not academics.

American Institute for Economic Research (AIER) — Publishes accessible articles on monetary policy, inflation, economic freedom, and everyday economics. Their Sound Money Project is particularly relevant to the ideas in Parts 7 and 8 of this book. *aier.org*

Cato Institute — A policy research organization that produces books, policy papers, podcasts, and events on economics, individual liberty, and limited government. *cato.org*

EconLib (Library of Economics and Liberty) — One of the best free resources for economic education. Features the Concise Encyclopedia of Economics, classic texts, and EconTalk — a podcast hosted by Russ Roberts where economists discuss ideas in plain language. EconTalk alone is worth your time. *econlib.org*

Foundation for Economic Education (FEE) — One of the oldest economic education organizations in the country. Produces articles, videos, and courses designed for students and general audiences. Their video content on YouTube is a great visual companion to the ideas in this book. FEE also publishes "I, Pencil," recommended in the reading list above. *fee.org*

Independent Institute — Produces books, articles, and policy research. Their approach bridges economics and public policy with an emphasis on practical solutions. Several of their publications — including *Choice* by Robert Murphy and Donald Boudreaux, recommended in the reading list above — are among the most accessible introductions to the ideas in this book. *independent.org*

Institute for Humane Studies (IHS) — Supports students and early-career scholars interested in the ideas of a free society. Offers seminars, discussion groups, and online content. If this book sparked a deeper interest and you want to explore these ideas in a community setting, IHS is a strong starting point. *theihs.org*

Learn Liberty — A video-based educational platform with short, well-produced explainers on economics, philosophy, and policy. If you prefer watching to reading, start here. *learnliberty.org*

Marginal Revolution University (MRU) — Free economics courses taught by Tyler Cowen and Alex Tabarrok of George Mason University. The Everyday Economics series covers many of the same topics as this book in short video format. Excellent for visual learners who want more depth. *mru.org*

Mercatus Center at George Mason University — A research center that bridges academic economics and public policy. Their policy briefs and working papers are more technical than this book, but their blog posts, podcasts, and short videos are accessible. Many of the economists whose ideas informed this book are affiliated with Mercatus. *mercatus.org*

Mises Institute — Publishes books, articles, lectures, and courses in the Austrian economics tradition. Their library of free books and audio content is enormous. *mises.org*

Reason Foundation — Publishes Reason magazine and Reason TV, covering economics, policy, and culture. Their video content is engaging and covers topics from occupational licensing to housing policy in an accessible, often entertaining format. *reason.org*

State Policy Network (SPN) — A national network of state-level policy research organizations — including Nevada Policy Institute, where I serve as a Senior Policy Fellow. If you want to see economic thinking applied to the issues in your own state, SPN's directory can connect you to your local organization. These groups produce articles, reports, and events that translate the principles in this book into real policy conversations happening in your community. *spn.org*

About The Author

Cameron M. Belt is an economist and business strategist. He believes economics is the most useful science for your life, business, and community that most people don't know how to use. After earning his M.A. in Economics from the University of Nevada, Reno, he spent six years as a regional executive at Lyft and Uber before transitioning to economic consulting and research. He currently serves as Senior Economist at RCG Economics, Senior Policy Fellow with Nevada Policy Institute, and Founding Partner of FLO Technology. Cameron has spent over a decade translating economic ideas into insights and actions for businesses and policymakers. He lives with his wife Amber and two dogs, Bear and Goldie, in Las Vegas, Nevada.

www.ingramcontent.com/pod-product-compliance
Lightning Source LLC
LaVergne TN
LVHW010717061126
851857LV00014B/1227
* 9 7 9 8 9 9 6 6 0 1 7 0 7 *